Selling the Old-Time Religion

Selling the Old-Time Religion

American Fundamentalists and Mass Culture, 1920–1940

Douglas Carl Abrams

The University of Georgia Press
Athens and London

© 2001 by the University of Georgia Press
Athens, Georgia 30602
All rights reserved

Designed by Erin Kirk New
Set in 10 on 14 Sabon by G & S Typesetters
Printed and bound by Thomson-Shore

The paper in this book meets the guidelines for permanence
and durability of the Committee on Production Guidelines for
Book Longevity of the Council on Library Resources.

Printed in the United States of America
05   04   03   02   01   C   5   4   3   2   1

Library of Congress Cataloging-in-Publication Data

Abrams, Douglas Carl, 1950–
    Selling the old-time religion : American fundamentalists and mass
    culture, 1920–1940 / Douglas Carl Abrams.
        p.   cm.
    Includes bibliographical references and index.
    ISBN 0-8203-2294-6 (alk. paper)
    1. Religious fundamentalism—United States—History.   I. Title.

    BR526.A27 2001
    277.3'082—dc21   2001017152

British Library Cataloging-in-Publication Data available

to Jessica and Benjamin,

children of the covenant

It was that old mass yearning for a likeness in all things that troubled them, and him. Neither his father nor his mother was like other people, because they were always making so much of religion, and now at last they were making a business of it.

Theodore Dreiser, *An American Tragedy* (1925)

Contents

Preface

The idea for this study developed from the influence of three books, all very different. George M. Marsden's *Fundamentalism and American Culture* (1980), with its broad cultural analysis, transcended the older theological and denominational approaches to fundamentalism and elevated the subject to a level of seriousness not seen before in studies that had dismissed it as an anachronism. The amount and quality of scholarship on fundamentalism since 1980 is due in part to the influence of that book. My debt to those historical studies is evident in my notes. Also in the course of pursuing my other interest, southern history, I encountered Daniel J. Singal's *The War Within* (1982), which examined how secular southern intellectuals made the transition from Victorianism to modernism during the 1920s and 1930s. The thought occurred to me that fundamentalists could be studied profitably from a similar premise. As a graduate student at the University of Maryland and a teaching assistant for the late Horace Samuel Merrill, I was intrigued by a book that he introduced to students one day—Bruce Barton's *The Man Nobody Knows* (1925). Indirectly, this study is an effort to understand that book, since Barton epitomized the merger of religion and business in the 1920s.

This work is intended for scholars and general readers interested in the topic. Although I have tried to be objective and even critical as a historian, let me acknowledge that my critique of modern culture and fundamentalism is colored by the fact that I am writing about a tradition that is my own.

My study is not a narrative history of fundamentalism; it does not explore its theology or role in politics during the interwar period. It is an examination of fundamentalist attitudes toward two aspects of modern life not treated before in book-length works—the consumer society and popular culture, both facets of mass culture that share elements of promotion. This work delves into how fundamentalists not only distinguished themselves from modern mass culture but also participated in it, making them less the "outsiders" in American society. Although their affinity for business is not a surprise, the degree of enthusiasm and what it reveals about fundamentalism is remarkable. Likewise, no one doubts their disdain for worldly pleasures, but the manner in which they borrowed its technologies and strategies is noteworthy. The result helps explain conservative evangelicalism's resilience over the decades. In the era of the Scopes Trial, when observers and later historians discounted the movement, fundamentalism adapted to the ways of middle-class America and thrived. In the end they imitated mass culture, not to be like the world but to evangelize it.

In this study both elites and lay people play an important role. The elites are more visible as leaders of the movement, and selections from manuscript collections, sermons, articles, and books form a large part of the text; however, the lay presence is also relatively strong. In dozens of places in the text, businesspeople, students and faculty of fundamentalist colleges and Bible schools, consumers, radio listeners, periodical readers, and women offer their grass-roots perspectives on mass culture. Fundamentalist organizations, operating mainly outside denominations, gave greater opportunities for laypeople. Periodical research is a good way to get a feel for the lay point of view, and my research in the periodicals is extensive—three major geographically representative magazines, plus selected others, covering two decades. As much as possible, I wanted fundamentalists to speak for themselves; surprisingly, they spoke in ways that touched on gender and class. Mixed with their hellfire and damnation rhetoric was some Madison Avenue and show business savvy. Describing their efforts as "selling the old-time religion" would be, to them, high praise.

A nineteenth-century gospel song, author unknown, asks nonbelievers the question "Have You Any Room for Jesus?" and in a later verse concedes that the world has "Room for pleasure, room for business," but not for "Christ the Crucified." Many fundamentalists also could have pleaded guilty to those misplaced priorities as well during the 1920s and 1930s.

Many generous people and organizations have helped make this work possible, and I thank them all. The project began with a National Endowment for the Humanities Summer Seminar with William R. Hutchison at Harvard Divinity School. Subsequent grants from the American Council of Learned Societies, the Historical Commission of the Southern Baptist Convention, and the Institute for the Study of American Evangelicals at Wheaton College made the research possible.

Special thanks go to Keith Olson, not only for reading the manuscript, but also for his tireless assistance over the years. Support from George Tindall helped with numerous grant applications. Daniel Turner, in addition to reading the manuscript, allowed me to use his oral history interviews, for which I am grateful. I also thank Virginia Brereton and two outside readers for the University of Georgia Press for reading and critiquing the manuscript at various stages. Their suggestions greatly improved the manuscript, and errors that remain are my responsibility alone. I am indebted to Malcolm Call of the University of Georgia Press for his support for the manuscript throughout the publication process.

For their gracious assistance I would like to thank the staffs of the following libraries and archives: Billy Graham Center and Buswell Library, both at Wheaton College, Moody Bible Institute, Westminster Seminary, Southern Baptist Historical Library and Archives, Library of Congress, State Historical Society of Wisconsin, and Bob Jones University Archives and Mack Library. Special thanks go to Patricia LeMaster at the Mack Library for her assistance with interlibrary loan requests. I thank Shelby Morris for help with proofreading.

As I have tried to blend faith and history, I would like to thank Michael Barrett, Ronald Horton, and Edward Panosian for being models of Christian scholarship. Gratitude also goes to J. W. Long Jr. for his direction at an important time. Special thanks go to Gary and Pat Johnson for introducing me and my family to Africa and to my friends in Kenya and South Africa for showing me that faith transcends culture.

Family, in the end, is most important. I am grateful to my late parents, Glenn and Edna Abrams, for the nurture that made this book possible. I am indebted to Nell Perry and the late Robert Perry, my wife's parents, for special encouragement beyond the call of duty over the years. Many thanks go to my oldest brother, Bobby, and his wife, Janice, for making my "shady, green pastures" richer and sweeter. I dedicate this book to my daughter, Jessica, and to my son, Benjamin. They remind me constantly of what is really important. To describe Linda—wife, best friend, historian, gourmet cook—I cannot improve on Proverbs 31:28: "Her children arise up, and call her blessed; her husband also, and he praiseth her."

Selling the Old-Time Religion

Introduction

In its obituary of John Roach Straton, the pastor of New York's Calvary Baptist Church during the 1920s, the *New Republic* labeled him the "Fundamentalist Pope" of New York City. Noting his old-time religion, yet his skyscraper church and use of radio, it summed up the man: "In spirit, he was a Baptist of the old school . . . in technique, he was a New Yorker of the twentieth century." This leading minister of the city for that decade, a "tall, gaunt, severe, country-bred clergyman," in the words of one historian, seemed an odd fit for the city at that time.[1]

Similarly, fundamentalists between World War I and World War II had a complicated relationship with modern society. Those architects of the movement fought a war with the secular world on several fronts, and although the theological one has been the most noted, there were others. Tension between religion and culture, a vital theme in western civilization, prevailed also within the minds of early fundamentalists. Christians in previous ages had wrestled with Greek philosophy, monarchy, or feudalism, and conservative Protestantism had, according to sociologist James D. Hunter, "its own unique encounter with the process of modernization."[2]

Fundamentalists responded ambiguously to mass culture between the wars. Tastes of the American masses, whether in consumption or in entertainment, forced those religious traditionalists to reject or accept certain features of modern, urban, industrial America. In the end they selectively sorted through the challenges to their values. As an antimodern movement, fundamentalism was rife with contradictions and tensions, reflecting both innovation and traditionalism. Although militantly antimodernist in theology and philosophy, this religious movement, with its obvious super-natural and mystical qualities, responded less resolutely to key features of technology, urbanization, efficiency, bureaucracy, mass-marketing, and leisure. They often adapted the forms of mass culture but rejected the substance. In that sense, it typified antimodernism in America. Historian Jackson Lears has concluded that antimodernism was ambivalent, "a complex blend of accommodation and protest," and "antimodern dissenters could half-consciously help to create a sleeker modern culture they neither understood nor desired." Fundamentalists, therefore, could be modern in vital ways, without the modernist temper.[3]

One facet of mass culture, consumption, blended well with the evangelical spirit, encountering only slight resistance from fundamentalists, most notably in the 1930s. Hard work that brought material success indicated God's blessing. Evangelism, like advertising, involved persuasion and making choices, and hopefully it yielded emotional satisfaction. In fact, their enthusiasm for the new business ethos was so marked that they could be cited as part creators of the twentieth-century consumer society. They sought to participate in the new democratic opportunity to consume, once the prerogative of the wealthy, and skillfully used advertising and promotion techniques, emphasized growth, and marketed through magazines and radio. Though Christ warned against the impossibility of believers' serving God and mammon (riches), fundamentalists welded material and spiritual values. Biblical virtues of patience, contentment, self-denial, and generosity yielded ground to materialism and immediate gratification. One measure of fundamentalist accommodation to the business ethos was their quiet, sometimes favorable, reaction to Bruce Barton's best-seller *The Man Nobody Knows,* which merged religion with the commercial spirit of the 1920s.[4]

By the early twentieth century, consumerism, for some, involved more than materialism or consumption of merchandise. According to Rodney Clapp, it "entails most profoundly the cultivation of pleasure, the pursuit of novelty, and the chasing after illusory experiences associated with material goods." The modern business ethos, therefore, is linked to popular culture, the realm of leisure. British sociologist Colin Campbell, in fact, has connected consumerism, what he terms "self-illusory hedonism," with religion and romanticism. Although he perhaps downplays the material world too much, his point is helpful in understanding religion and consumption. Puritans, he argued, far from being "emotionally impoverished," had "most intense but controlled passion." Religious introspection, gauging the authenticity of their faith, rendered them emotionally sensitive, and religious emotions became a source of pleasure. Religious orthodoxy waned, but the romantic era preserved this emotional emphasis, and in a modern secular society consumerism and leisure provide similar emotional satisfaction. Advertising, with its images, imagination, passion, and exotic, idealized qualities, joined romanticism and consumerism.[5]

Campbell further argued that romantic and Puritan values can be balanced and integrated. Rather than being a contradiction or a tension, the Puritan and romantic character ideals can be incorporated into one personality. These apparently opposite cultural traditions are the "single cultural system of modernity"; they help sustain industrial society, "matching consumption with production, play with work."[6]

Fundamentalists illustrate this ambiguity in their reaction to popular culture in the 1920s and 1930s. They sensed threats to youth and home. Of course, they denounced liquor, cigarettes, gambling, and dancing, and most condemned the urban evils of theater and movies. Radio, jazz, magazines, and novels proved troublesome, and for many the flapper, the new woman of the era, embodied various aspects of decadent popular culture. The lures of secular entertainment, however, divided fundamentalists. Some roundly condemned popular culture, whereas others, though repelled by its vulgarities, were attracted to its forms and technologies and adapted them to church and evangelism. The church and Christian college, bulwarks against the onslaughts of secular pleasures, provided a subculture where faith and pleasure were united on fundamentalist terms.

Close scrutiny of fundamentalists and mass culture for the interwar years reveals a remarkable complexity. While embracing the marketing devices of the consumer society to spread the gospel, fundamentalists gave religious sanction to such secular strategies as advertising, important to modernization. They rejected certain leisure activities as threats to their holiness yet imitated these activities, and in the process they accommodated partially to America's growing therapeutic culture, which valued happiness above all.

Their embrace of mass culture highlights a paradoxical relationship between religion and materialism. Looking at materialism in a general sense, Robert Wuthnow has observed that the lines between the spiritual and material worlds, both part of Western civilization, had been blurred by advertising, with its manipulation of images. Consequently our spirituality has been "domesticated," he continued, by materialism. "Our religious impulses, therefore, caution us against becoming too materialistic, but their prompting is limited because we are thoroughly embedded in a world of material goods." Colleen McDannell has argued that there must be a "new religious configuration" for the twentieth century. In the tension between religion and secularization, religion continues to thrive by changing into something "new." In a study of Christians and religious material objects, she concluded that Christians blended the sacred and secular at the popular level, and that the "scrambling of the sacred and the profane is common in American Christianity." Likewise, fundamentalists, some who consciously argued against separating the sacred and the secular, proved resilient through adaptability to modern techniques.[7] Though fundamentalists had this affinity for the secular, they ironically shared with liberal Protestants and some secular intellectuals an ambivalence toward mass culture. All had enthusiasm for, yet misgivings about, the consumer society and popular culture. In fact, both fundamentalists and liberal Protestants may have been marginal to modernist culture, the former being more modern and the latter more Victorian than heretofore recognized. Daryl G. Hart has pointed out that one leading fundamentalist, J. Gresham Machen, feared modern Protestant theologians and their threat more than cultural modernists and secular literary and artistic intellectuals. Machen may not have been alone. Their accommodation to consumption and pleasure may have led them to underestimate the dangers of secular, modern culture. Although they defended the fundamentals of the faith from liberal attacks, these traditionalists, as quintessential middle-class Americans, participated in mass culture that forever changed them, for better and worse.[8]

Fundamentalists' relationship to mass culture may also help explain their success. Historian Edward J. Larson has concluded that the modern Scopes Trial legend, "portraying the . . . trial as a decisive defeat for old-time religion," started with the 1931 publication of the best-seller

Only Yesterday: An Informal History of the Nineteen-Twenties, written by journalist Frederick Lewis Allen. For half a century the book influenced historians who repeated Allen's "presentation of fundamentalism as a vanquished foe." Rather than disappearing, fundamentalists built thriving institutions in the interwar years by focusing on evangelism and spreading the gospel. Joel A. Carpenter concluded that "Their goals were time-honored evangelical ones: to bring revival to America and the gospel to the world," and by tapping into mass culture they were "retooling revivalism." Michael S. Hamilton, in his study of Wheaton College, has asserted that evangelism, not militance or premillennialism, should define fundamentalism. They tapped modern techniques for an old-fashioned reason, evangelism. Without denominational support they had to build grass-roots organizations, relying on popular, volunteer, lay support. "Fundamentalist entrepreneurs," Hamilton observed, "used the press, radio, and summer Bible conferences to appeal directly to lay people for support." "Fundamentalism," he added, "has always lashed itself to the raft of popular culture, and therefore changes in popular culture—those that do not strike against irreducible evangelical essentials—often produce corresponding changes in fundamentalism." They used modern mass culture to evangelize, and that adaptation did alter their strategies, but not their orthodox beliefs.[9]

Fundamentalism is an elusive term, but historian George Marsden has delineated its critical features: "Militant opposition to modernism was what most clearly set off fundamentalism from a number of closely related traditions," and as a movement it was a "loose, diverse, and changing federation of co-belligerents united by their fierce opposition to modernist attempts to bring Christianity into line with modern thought." He identified dispensational premillennialism, which divided history into specific dispensations, or epochs, with history culminating in Christ's return and his thousand-year reign on earth, as a critical fundamentalist tradition. Other important traditions were the holiness movement, defense of the faith, revivalism, and concerns about secular culture. Clearly a militant attitude toward liberal Protestantism distinguished a fundamentalist from fellow conservative Protestants and evangelicals. Distinguishing a fundamentalist in a cultural setting, however, is a more difficult task than defining one in a theological or ecclesiastical context. Separating them culturally from middle-class Americans at the time is often tricky. In fact, one scholar studying economics and contemporary fundamentalists concluded, "It simply is not possible to survey a representative sample of fundamentalists as distinct from other theologically conservative Protestants." Its nature as a popular movement makes a definition of fundamentalism even more difficult. In the interwar period, and in this study, *fundamentalist* and *conservative Protestant* or *evangelical* were often interchangeable terms, which only adds to the fluid nature of the movement.[10]

Placing fundamentalists in a historical context, however, sharpens their identity. The movement known by the early twentieth century as fundamentalism originated in late-nineteenth-century revivalism, typified by evangelist Dwight L. Moody. This revivalism was interdenominational and centered in the cities of the Northeast and upper Midwest. Certain key beliefs and practices characterized this emerging Protestant group: evangelism to save souls was paramount; holiness required believers to be pure and filled with the Holy Spirit in order to serve God; dispensational premillennialism focused on the imminent return of Christ; and the Bible was inspired by God and free from error.[11]

By the early twentieth century the developing movement grew increasingly resistant to liberal Protestant theology and the secularization of American life. *The Fundamentals,* twelve booklets published between 1910 and 1915, codified fundamentalist beliefs and complaints, but World War I revolutionized their view of American culture. Fearful that modernism would do to America what it had already done to Germany, fundamentalists grew militant and in 1919 organized the World's Christian Fundamentals Association (WCFA), and in 1920, Curtis Lee Laws, editor of the Baptist *Watchman-Examiner,* coined the label *fundamentalist* for his militant brethren. Fundamentalists fought losing battles with modernists in the Northern Baptist Convention and the (northern) Presbyterian Church in the United States, and as the militancy escalated, many conservatives left the cause. By the 1930s their coalition was not as broad as before, but the fundamentalist movement remained the most powerful force in evangelicalism.[12] Evangelicals often shared some of the same goals as fundamentalists but could not be considered part of the movement for what some might consider subtle, but nonetheless important, reasons. As Joel Carpenter observed, "Fundamentalists are evangelicals, but not all evangelicals are fundamentalists." Southern Baptists, for example, were conservative and evangelistic in the 1920s and 1930s but not fundamentalist because that movement was too premillennial, too interdenominational, and, for some, too militant. Pentecostal and holiness groups also shared similar instincts with fundamentalists, but the latter resented holiness and Pentecostal teachings about faith healing and speaking in tongues. Furthermore, fundamentalists were more involved in rescuing American culture.[13]

Diversity among fundamentalists precluded a uniform response to modernity. Pastors, evangelists, professors, administrators, and journalists all perceived its impact with shades of differences. Baptist pastors—John Roach Straton, William Bell Riley of First Baptist Church in Minneapolis, Jasper Cortenus (J. C.) Massee of Tremont Temple in Boston, and J. Frank Norris of First Baptist Church in Ft. Worth and, after 1935, simultaneously pastor of Temple Baptist Church in Detroit—formed a core of the movement. The Reformed wing, however, proved influential as well: Presbyterians J. Gresham Machen of Princeton and later Westminster Seminary, James Oliver Buswell, president of Wheaton College, Charles G. Trumbull, *Sunday School Times* editor, evangelist Billy Sunday, pastors Mark Matthews of Seattle and Clarence Macartney of Pittsburgh, layman and political leader William Jennings Bryan; also Congregationalist Reuben A. Torrey, pastor, evangelist, and Bible teacher, and James M. Gray, Reformed Episcopalian, president of Moody Bible Institute, and editor of *Moody Monthly*. Robert Shuler of Trinity Methodist Church in Los Angeles and Bob Jones Sr., evangelist and founder of Bob Jones College, represented the minority Methodist presence. Evangelist-pastor Paul Rader typified the interdenominational nature of the movement. Although fundamentalists agreed on the essentials of conservative Protestantism, such as the inspiration of scripture, the Creation, the deity of Christ, the Atonement, the Resurrection, and the New Birth, they had theological and denominational differences. Fundamentalists were Arminians and Calvinists. Some favored local church government; others insisted on highly centralized church polity. Methodists and Presbyterians baptized infants by sprinkling, as a sign of the covenant; Baptists administered the rite by immersing believers, as a symbol of the new birth.

Fundamentalists also disagreed about political and social issues. The movement's core was Republican, but southerners, along with leading spokesperson William Jennings Bryan, were Democrats. Most, but not all, fundamentalists engaged in social causes, such as fighting liquor and evolution. Most looked for Christ's return to usher in the millennium, while others pursued spiritual and social progress that would lead to a millennium first and then the return of Christ. They also disagreed about cultural issues. Some fundamentalists did not endorse all facets of the business ethos and criticized specifically advertising techniques and the idolizing of efficiency. Likewise, some shunned modern forms of popular culture, such as drama and film, as inherently evil. Most fundamentalists, of course, embraced elements of secular culture, whether in commerce or in amusements.[14]

Fundamentalists built a variety of organizations and bureaucracies, as did secular modern Americans. "Empires" included large urban churches, periodicals—*Sunday School Times, Moody Monthly,* and *King's Business*—with a national audience, institutions of higher education—Wheaton College and Bob Jones College—and Bible colleges such as Moody Bible Institute, Northwestern Schools, and the Bible Institute of Los Angeles (BIOLA).

Ethnically, most fundamentalists were Anglo-Americans or Protestants of northern European immigrant background. Although they cut across class lines and included skilled and unskilled workers, farmers, businesspeople, clerks, and owners of large and small companies, the general pattern was middle to lower-middle class and the "better" working class. Fundamentalists tended to be younger and newer arrivals in the community than mainline Protestants. Faith, evangelism, and religious community, however, were far more important than identification with social class.[15]

Geographically, fundamentalism was a national movement. Long viewed as a rural phenomenon, it thrived in America's great urban centers—New York, Philadelphia, Pittsburgh, Boston, Detroit, Chicago, Minneapolis, Ft. Worth, Los Angeles, and Seattle—where commerce and entertainment had a greater presence. Strongest in the mid-Atlantic and Midwest, it also had significant followers in New England and on the West Coast. Traditionally cast as a stronghold for militant Protestantism, the South produced only two resident southerners as major leaders between the wars—J. Frank Norris and Bob Jones Sr. A region with less strident modernism meant a diminished fundamentalist response in organizational terms. However, the South did produce an impressive number of figures who spearheaded the cause beyond its borders, and the anti-evolution movement brought fundamentalism into the public arena. Several men, born in the region and shaped by its conservative religious and social values, transported those views to urban America: Shuler in Los Angeles, Matthews in Seattle, Massee in Boston, and Straton, who spent formative years in the South, in New York City. Riley and Machen, through their parents, carried the imprint of the region.[16]

As a group, fundamentalist leaders were well educated. In an age when a high school diploma placed an American in an educated elite, several of the men had advanced degrees. Machen and Torrey finished their education with European studies after degrees from Johns Hopkins and Yale, respectively. Riley, Norris, Massee, Buswell, and Macartney completed college and seminary, whereas Shuler and Jones attended college. Their training enabled them to meet the challenge of modern culture in a worldly-wise fashion. They recognized facets of modernity that were inimical to faith and that had to be opposed, and they also discerned aspects that could be adapted to the mission to advance the kingdom of Christ. They grasped the Apostle John's admonition to "Love not the world" (1 John 2:15) but intuitively understood the ambiguity in the Apostle Paul's declaration: "I am made all things to all men, that I might by all means save some" (1 Cor. 9:22).

The interwar period was a critical one for fundamentalism. That era produced the founding fathers of the movement, the first generation of self-designated fundamentalist leaders, who organized for the battle against modernism. This religious community had solidified by the early 1930s. Secular events both startled them and drew their interest. Like most Americans, they had an affinity for conservative Republican politics and enjoyed the prosperity of the 1920s, but they showed little enthusiasm for the New Deal as a remedy for the depression. Cultural changes revolutionized American life. Technology led the way: an affordable automobile, movies with sound, advances in aviation, surging interest in sports, and innovations in publishing. While conservatives sought to maintain prohibition and feared communist and immigrant influences, others challenged tradition. Women, armed with suffrage, pushed for more rights, and some questioned Victorian mores. Popular modern ideas, such as Freudian psychology, filtered into mainstream America. Modernist literature and jazz overturned previous cultural certainties. African Americans migrated in great numbers from the rural South to the urban North and Midwest and contributed to the new social mosaic.[17]

No longer aloof to the perils of American culture, fundamentalists were now seriously disturbed about them. They crusaded against one modern notion, evolution, but the 1925 Scopes Trial embarrassed them. Hard work continued, however, with the 1928 presidential campaign against Al Smith, an antiprohibitionist and a Catholic, and, more importantly, with the building of fundamentalist institutions. By the early 1930s a committed remnant of the fundamentalist movement remained. Despite the enormous political, economic, and social changes of the interwar period, fundamentalists persisted in their mission. The unity of these militant evangelicals for these two decades stands in contrast to the movement's splintering in the 1940s and 1950s over the issue of separation from liberal Protestants. After World War II conservative Protestantism consisted of evangelicals, who wearied of confrontation, and fundamentalists, who remained militant.[18]

1

Embracing the Consumer Society

Charles A. Blanchard's funeral in 1925 provided a signal moment for fundamentalism. William Bell Riley, perhaps the movement's premier spokesperson at that time, delivered the eulogy. He noted that Blanchard loved first his family and second Wheaton College, where he had served as president from 1882 to 1925. Blanchard, as much as anyone, symbolized evangelicalism's transition from a nineteenth-century emphasis on revival and reform to early-twentieth-century fundamentalism. He had known Dwight L. Moody, and his ministry spanned until after World War I, when he helped Riley found the World's Christian Fundamentals Association (WCFA).[1]

In his remarks Riley chose not to highlight Blanchard's roles as educator, reformer, or spiritual leader. Instead he tapped the idiom that his audience would understand as the highest praise for the 1920s by underscoring Blanchard's business ability. Admiring Wheaton's faculty, board of directors, buildings, and endowment, Riley praised Blanchard as a "man of affairs, far-seeing and efficient." Blanchard, unlike the common impression of ministers, did have a business sense. The "biggest affairs . . . on the face of the earth," including the church, have been "inaugurated and put through by ministers," declared Riley.[2]

In the 1920s and 1930s, fundamentalists energetically embraced the business ethos with its secular values of organization, efficiency, consumerism, promotionalism, and emphasis on size and numbers. To evangelize and build institutions, they tapped innovative modern strategies and technologies, such as advertising, magazines, and radio. So considerable was the adaptation that they complained little about the writings of Bruce Barton, the "high priest" of the consumer society. They had made some peace with what David S. Reynolds called "the new America, the America of huge corporations, machines, robber barons, advertising agencies, department stores, and rampant consumerism." Criticism of business, minimal during the 1920s, increased only slightly during the depression. When President Coolidge in a famous dictum of the 1920s compared a factory to a temple and its workers to worshippers, he reflected an affinity between business and religion that fundamentalists also celebrated, sometimes to embarrassing extremes. A. C. Dixon, pastor, evangelist, and the first editor of *The Fundamentals,* a series of volumes published between 1910 and 1915 that defined the movement, had argued even earlier against a "too clear-cut distinction between business and religion." "Let him [the businessman] wipe out the word 'secular' from his vocabulary. He is God's steward, and now his office becomes sacred as a church; his ledger is as holy as his Bible, for both are God's books. . . . Monday he hallows by opening his store . . . so that it, too, becomes a sanctuary of service." [3]

Fundamentalists made a thoroughgoing connection to business in the era. They related to all types of business: small shop, department store, factory, and huge corporation. Paradoxically, the type they emulated most often, the corporation, was generally the one they attacked, when on rare occasions they did criticize business. Their embrace of commerce included both its rhetoric and practice. This blend of enterprise and faith involved some businesspeople who became fundamentalist preachers and laypeople who showcased their faith while remaining successful businesspeople; both groups reveled in commercialism.

Not surprisingly, a general identity of business with religion pervaded the rhetoric of fundamentalism in the early decades of the twentieth century. The church "is a business as constant and engaging as is that in a department store," Riley pointed out to readers of a religious periodical. Curtis Laws, a Baptist editor who coined the label *fundamentalist,* visited Riley in Minneapolis and, after seeing the three-thousand-member church with its million-dollar property, agreed: "The whole church edifice seemed to me to be bustling with life like a great department store." A less devout observer of Riley described him as "the pre-occupied businessman, with a thousand things on his mind." This visitor criticized his impersonal, restless office demeanor, sighs mixed with dictation: "He will hurry through the conversation and send you out to make way" for the next visitor.[4]

Other leaders of the movement linked faith and enterprise. J. C. Massee declared that "the business of winning men to Christ is the most taxing and exhausting business on earth. . . . Soul-winning is big business." Evangelist William E. Biederwolf, agreeing with Massee, commented that the church's "business" of recruiting men and women to Christ was comparable to the automobile factory's business of manufacturing automobiles. An admirer of Reuben A. Torrey, a protégé of Dwight L. Moody's, memorialized him by suggesting that he "could easily have been the dominant executive head of some large corporation." In 1922 a reporter proclaimed thirty-eight-year-old evangelist Bob Jones to be "one of the Hardest Hitting Men in the Business." With his "snappy" style, Jones had convinced him that he had made an "unusually close study of his business."[5]

Business and religion were not just for men. Women were critical to the emerging consumer culture as major purchasers. One female writer in the *Sunday School Times,* explaining "How a Christian Business Girl Gets Her Work Done," noted that the "very first Christian in Europe was a business woman, 'Lydia, a seller of purple,'" and reassured readers that Jesus Christ was "practical" for the office. Women had to cease their exclusive focus on activities for Christ and had to prepare spiritually for the office by having a devotional "Quiet Time" in the morning. The result would be a "new spirit" in the office: "Giving the Lord the first hour, He takes charge of her whole day."[6]

Periodicals also magnified the affinity of religion for business. An ad in the *Moody Monthly* announced that the Bible was "The World's First Business Book." To attract students to the Moody Bible Institute correspondence courses, the ad described the Bible as a "complete business library" that "answered fundamentally every one of today's business problems." Charles A. Tawney, a Pennsylvania bank president writing in the pages of the predecessor of *Moody Monthly,* asked the question with a self-evident answer: "do you realize that there is really only one important business in the world, and that is Christian gospel work?" He quoted David's words in 1 Samuel 21:8 and, with a bit of tortured exegesis, furthered the connection to commerce: "the king's business requireth haste."[7]

The fundamentalist periodical with the most enthusiasm for capitalism, it seemed, was the *King's Business,* published monthly since 1910 by the Bible Institute of Los Angeles (BIOLA). "BUSINESS FOR THE KING," its editor announced in 1924, is the "greatest business in all the world." In 1926 the editorial page carried a reprint of the magazine's editorial in the first issue in 1910, which extolled business. The writer argued that the Lord was a businessman, and in the gospel parable of the pounds, the nobleman as a type of Christ had commanded the servants to "Occupy (do business) till I come." The editor concluded that "The supreme business in this world is that which a loving Lord has committed to His servants— the giving of the glorious Gospel to a perishing people."[8]

Those associated with the *King's Business,* a "proto-fundamentalist periodical" according to historian Mark A. Noll, accepted as a given, as did many other fundamentalists, that businessmen intuitively understood spiritual need, perhaps better than others, so therefore the business ethos was appropriate for the gospel. Reverend T. C. Horton, editor of the periodical, Presbyterian Bible teacher, and participant in the founding of BIOLA, quoted favorably such men as Richard H. Edmonds, editor of the *Manufacturer's Record,* and economist Roger Babson when they prescribed religion as the need for America in the early 1920s. "We do not know whether they are Christians or not but we do know that they have hit the nail squarely on the head." Since they were "sound, practical businessmen," Edmonds and Babson deserved hearing. Then Horton, in a contradictory manner, added that "20th century methods of Christian work" would not solve the problem either. Only "God's ordained means," preaching the gospel, was the solution. Still, Horton and others did not disdain modern methods to spread that gospel. Two years later Horton reiterated that businessmen "recognized that the ideals of Christ must be realized in human life and in business life, if prosperity and peace are to be maintained." He challenged businessmen to go beyond ideals to preach Christ and the Word, the only real solution. "His word works today in shop and factory, in store and school."[9]

Fundamentalist alliance with capitalism derived from a distinct heritage, popularized in the nineteenth century by sociologist Max Weber, who tied a Protestant work ethic to industrialization. Even if the connection was overdrawn generally, it may be an apt one for late-nineteenth-century American evangelicals, fundamentalism's predecessors, as historian Douglas W. Frank noted. Economic striving paralleled Calvinism. Middle-class evangelicals viewed hard work and financial success as signs of divine approbation. The Calvinist, the evangelical, maintained an inner spiritual order, which enabled him to bring order to the business life, important for middle-class industrial society.[10]

In the late nineteenth century evangelist Dwight L. Moody exhibited the unity of religion and business by adapting recent business innovations to urban revivalism. Moody, a businessman himself before becoming an evangelist, so blended evangelism, enterprise, and mass culture that historian James Gilbert credits him with participating in "creating modern commercial culture." This fusion, although not new, was dramatic and particularly apt for Victorian and industrial culture in which striving in business relations resonated with spiritual quest.[11]

In the early twentieth century the dynamics of this relationship changed. Cultural authority had transferred from religion to commerce. Rather than being the authority for society, religion had become one of many commodities competing in a mass society. To regain their prestige in society, churches in the 1920s, both liberal and conservative, adapted to business culture. Never before had business and religion been joined in such a deliberate and self-conscious manner. Churches generally celebrated commercial values and did not confront materialism or the business ethos of the 1920s. The result, according to historian Rolf Lundén, was that the church looked like a "poor copy of the business world," business became a "pseudoreligion," and generally the economic order remained unchallenged.[12]

Over the decades evangelicals—and later, fundamentalists—had forged close ties with Christian businessmen. In 1829 brothers Arthur and Lewis Tappan, wealthy New York merchants, were converted under Charles Finney's ministry in the Second Great Awakening. Finney appealed especially to the wealthy, and their cooperation gave them a certain moral and social legitimacy, while the revivalist enjoyed financial support. In the nineteenth century the American Bible Society transformed itself from a primarily benevolent religious organization to a successful business when it shifted to agents to sell Bibles. Into the early twentieth century a mutual social, political, and economic conservatism persisted for some businessmen. A stronger orthodoxy might weaken the appeal of the social gospel and could discredit its critique of capitalism, and a patriotic faith could serve as a bulwark against socialism and Bolshevism, the archenemies for businessmen.[13]

Liberal Protestants had rich business connections also—for example, the Rockefeller association with Harry Emerson Fosdick's Riverside Church in New York City and the University of Chicago, a leading modernist seminary. Rockefeller, according to biographer Ron Chernow, "embodied the sometimes uneasy symbiosis between church and business that defined the emerging ethos of the post–Civil War American economy." Rockefeller's linking wealth and personal piety also anticipated similar fundamentalist attitudes. Still, that did not stop the unfounded conspiratorial charge by liberals in some quarters, started during World War I, that millions of dollars funded the premillennialism of fundamentalist leaders, in an effort to create a disinterest in reform and foreign policy. Rabbi Stephen Wise and journalist George Creel in 1923 accused Billy Sunday of being a tool of the industrialists for going to West Virginia for a revival campaign during a coal strike. The timing was coincidental but, at least for his enemies, reinforced Sunday's ties to businessmen like John D. Rockefeller Jr.[14]

Links to business were sufficient to give such attacks credibility, for fundamentalists had, in the words of historian R. Laurence Moore, "their own list of sugar-daddy businessmen." Amos K. Gordon, vice president of Standard Oil of Louisiana, supported Arno Gaebelein, editor of *Our Hope*, a leading dispensationalist periodical. Charles L. Huston, president of Philadelphia School of the Bible, was a prominent official in the Lukens Steel Company. Henry P. Crowell, chair of Quaker Oats, was also chair of the board of Moody Bible Institute. J. C. Penny contributed generously to fundamentalist causes. Wealthy contributors often sustained the ministry of William Bell Riley. Bob Jones Sr. in the summer of 1915 held a ten-day tent campaign in New York City, sponsored by millionaires. After he assumed a Detroit pastorate in 1935, while also retaining one in Ft. Worth,

Texas, J. Frank Norris befriended the presidents and vice presidents of the "Big Three" automakers, who provided loaner cars for his crusade travels. Even J. Gresham Machen, who shared Seal Harbor, Maine, with John D. Rockefeller Jr. as a summer home, once accepted his invitation to preach at the little village church, although Machen protested that he did not believe in uniting with men of differing views of the Christian religion.[15]

Two of the most revered Christian businessmen were John Wanamaker and Lyman Stewart. Wanamaker, a Presbyterian layman, leader in the Sunday School movement, and former owner and publisher of the *Sunday School Times,* pioneered in retailing in Philadelphia, relying on innovative modern advertising and the use of full-page newspaper ads beginning in 1899. This close friend of Moody's, who refused to sell alcohol in his department stores, made French fashions and other luxuries readily available to Americans and had the largest furniture showrooms in the country. He built the largest department store and presided over the largest Sunday school class in the country. In 1876, before he opened his Grand Depot, it was used by Moody for a camp meeting. According to his biographer, "His stores, like a large camp meeting, had an openness that attracted individuals to come, look around, listen, and make a decision." Wanamaker also contributed to the commercialization of Christmas and Easter by decking out his Philadelphia store with appropriate seasonal religious embellishments. Wanamaker referred to his stores as a "pulpit," and his twelve-story Philadelphia emporium, which opened in 1911, with its Grand Court, resembled a cathedral at Christmas with its pipe organ and caroling. According to cultural historian Leigh E. Schmidt, "During the holidays people did not just shop at Wanamaker's; they received devotional reminders and religious encouragement." Stewart, a pioneer in the oil industry in California, a Presbyterian layperson, and the founder and president of the Bible Institute of Los Angeles, sponsored along with his brother the publication of *The Fundamentals.* Wanamaker died in 1922 and Stewart the following year, as both the fundamentalist movement and the business civilization entered their peak period.[16]

Moreover, some fundamentalist leaders had business and industry backgrounds. George F. Washburn, organizer of Bible Crusaders of America and close to William Jennings Bryan, was a real estate dealer and owner of apartment buildings and a hotel chain. Mel Trotter, before going to

Grand Rapids, Michigan, in 1900 to start his rescue mission ministry, had been a barber, operated a barber supply business, and sold insurance. He was also an ordained Presbyterian minister and evangelist and had joined the Grand Rapids Rotary Club. Chicago pastor-evangelist Paul Rader had a varied career before the ministry, including stints in oil prospecting and public relations. Mordecai Ham, an evangelist under whom Billy Graham was converted, entered the grocery business briefly and then worked as a traveling salesperson in the Chicago area before turning to preaching. A young Billy Graham, during the summer before he entered Bob Jones College in the fall of 1936, sold Fuller brushes. He remembered later that some customers complained that "I was trying to give them a hard sell about Christ as much as about Fuller brushes."[17] Prior stints in business served as a source of pride for some, a virtual credential that enhanced success as a minister.

Fundamentalists identified with the business ethos more than in a general sense; specific aspects of it resonated with their thoughts and actions. By the late nineteenth century large organizations, economic, social, and governmental, had challenged the farm and small town for dominance in American life. As historian Robert Wiebe had argued, an impulse for organization pervaded American society as business led the way and other groups imitated the corporate world. In that turn-of-the-century world, business produced the big organizations, which served as models for churches and evangelism. The standard for religious success shifted somewhat from a spiritual one to one judged by the size of budgets and buildings and the number of members and converts. In 1923 the *Church Management* journal emerged to help pastors organize their church operations from attendance and Sunday school to finances and advertising. That fundamentalists would so specifically emulate the organizational emphasis of business has profound implications for their relationship to modernity, because sociologist James Davison Hunter has described a "rationalized economy as the primary determining carrier of modernization." By trying to be like business, therefore, fundamentalists had absorbed the vital aspect of modernity.[18]

This development was not new, for Dwight L. Moody earlier had borrowed from corporate organization in his evangelistic work, but fundamentalists in the 1920s pushed it further. The connection with business was more intense and universal, the overall emphasis greater. "Give me the right sort of organization and there will be no sinner left in a town at the close of one of my campaigns," Bob Jones Sr. boasted to a reporter during a Montgomery, Alabama, campaign in 1921. The reporter agreed that the evangelist based his "great soul saving process on a business-like foundation." J. C. Massee urged evangelists to adapt the methods of big business, with its emphasis on proper organization. Underlying this attraction to business was a desire for respectability. Just as businesspeople, doctors, lawyers, and other professionals had gained status with organization, so must evangelists. Increasingly, evangelists wanted to be viewed as professionals, providing a service like a physician, attorney, or pastor.[19]

William E. Biederwolf, general secretary of the Commission on Evangelism of the Federal Council of Churches, relished a blend of professionalism and organization for his calling. "They tell us to depend on the power of the Holy Spirit," Biederwolf responded to critics of organization—"As if the Holy Spirit appreciates incoherency and confusion more than he does unity and cooperation." He added that only a "most thorough organization" could promote a campaign. The successful evangelist, he contended, could not "lie down" as in Psalm 23, because the church had to keep pace with the population by increasing in size. Willis G. Haymaker, after honing his skills for twelve years as a revival campaign organizer for men like Billy Sunday, offered advice for a similar effort for evangelist Gypsy Smith in Stockton, California, in 1928. He required five to six weeks of advance work with various committees from finance, music, ushers, young people, entertainment, transportation, and publicity to handle numerous details, in addition to building the tabernacle. The cottage prayer meeting committee had the critical task of dividing the city into divisions and districts, with captains and lieutenants over each, respectively. In each district, about twenty to thirty homes were to hold prayer meetings from 10:00 to 10:30 A.M., Tuesday through Friday, weeks before the campaign. Haymaker believed that his plan of organization had proven effective.[20]

William Bell Riley utilized organization for a thriving pastorate. Just as every large business was organized, Riley insisted that for the church to

succeed in a city it had to use "intelligent methods": "The Church ought
to represent the corporate business of the Christians who worship in it,
and every method that is . . . destined to high success ought to be introduced." He followed his own advice and built the strongest fundamentalist "empire" in the Midwest, a network of churches spun off from his
Northwestern Bible School and First Baptist Church of Minneapolis. His
empire functioned similarly to a denomination, supplying pastors, starting churches, and controlling them. The WCFA, created in 1919 largely
through Riley's efforts, presented an alternative national organization to
the mainstream Federal Council of Churches. Riley pastored in Minneapolis from 1897 to 1942 and also was an active evangelist, debater, and
editor. Little wonder one historian has labeled him an "organizational
Fundamentalist."[21]

There were dissenting voices, some from the more pietistic tradition
within fundamentalism. R. A. Torrey spoke out against his brethren's bent
for the machinery of scientific management. Instead of organization, he
urged that believers focus on the Holy Spirit and the power needed for
service. One contributor to the *Sunday School Times* observed that machinery had a place in effective church work, but not the "chief place,"
which would make the minister "a manager of machinery instead of a
prophet of God. . . . A church must be spiritual first and foremost and
forever." Editor Charles G. Trumbull decried the "worship of bigness"
that has "fevered us all" and cautioned that the prophet Zechariah
"warned against despising the day of small things."[22]

Even some of those who at times embraced the organizational impulse
professed ambivalence about the consequences. Riley distrusted bureaucracy and organization at the same time that he and other fundamentalists
built huge bureaucracies of their own. He resisted efforts to professional-
ize or standardize the ministry. He felt that denominational hierarchy had
no right to insist on a college-educated clergy and that the standard should
be spiritual, not cultural. Although he criticized the Federal Council of
Churches for monopolistic practices akin to big business, he planned a
"confederacy" of his own that culminated in the WCFA. Even the *King's
Business,* a most fervent advocate of economic boosterism, sounded a
different note after the stock market crash and the hiring of a new edi-

tor: "What the church needs is not more machinery, or better; not new organizations, or more methods, but men whom the Holy Spirit can use."[23] Generally, however, fundamentalist enthusiasm for business continued during the Great Depression.

The Progressive Era, the years immediately preceding World War I, prized efficiency, a value important in American society but especially for business, with its potential for maximizing profits. Fundamentalists had vigorously embraced this major theme. Rescue mission builder Mel Trotter could declare about his Grand Rapids, Michigan, operation that saving souls was as practical as pawnbroking: "I have got our soul-saving reduced to as exact a business basis as any business is run. Last year our mission . . . largest . . . on the globe, brought in many hundreds of converts. It cost exactly $1.60 for every soul saved." Frederick W. Taylor, pioneer of scientific management in the early twentieth century, would have been pleased. The emphasis was contagious. "Christianity doesn't make people inefficient; it makes them efficient. . . . it makes them do everything better. It makes a man a better husband. . . . It makes a better businessman," expounded Bob Jones Sr. An observer praised Paul Rader's "instinctive knowledge of efficiency" and his "passion for the highest degree of efficiency to be applied in the Lord's work."[24]

An emphasis on efficiency permeated various ministries. Evangelists built large tabernacles, temporary structures, for urban revivals because of their advantages over city auditoriums, ranging from size, accessibility, acoustics, low cost, and novelty to the clean, bright, warm, and noiseless sawdust floor. Ministers had to use up-to-date labor-saving methods found in the modern business office: pocket reminders, desk calendars, typewriters, addressing machines, and a loose-leaf notebook for those troublesome sermon notes. Furthermore, the telephone could make the Sunday school more efficient. Teachers could contact absentees, the sick, new members, and last-minute substitute teachers.[25]

For many fundamentalists Bible schools provided Christian workers, particularly ministers, with more efficient training than a liberal arts college. The schools could be quicker and to the point, given their specialization, an often-cited word that resonated with their zest for business. R. A. Torrey criticized the self-educated or seminary-trained pastor as inadequate: "We live in an age of specialization in education." The need was for a "training school for evangelists," not a "milk-and-water college for general culture." [26]

Some fundamentalists resisted the scientific management ideals, an indication that, for some, the borrowing from the business ethos was more than innocent rhetoric; they viewed it as a threat to the very nature of the spiritual life. "There is too much dependence today on 'human efficiency' and too little dependence upon divine power," warned John Roach Straton, ironically one who had great zest for other modern techniques. One religious editor cited efficiency as the watchword of the day and called it desirable in the areas of engineering, science, and business. "But the one supreme need for the nation, as for the individual," he insisted, "is spiritual efficiency." For him spiritual efficiency meant conversions to Christ, the goal of preaching the gospel and evangelizing. J. Gresham Machen viewed efficiency more perniciously than others. The modern ideal, according to him, would be a world in which the human machine reached the highest stage of efficiency. The price for this drab, mechanistic world would be a loss of liberty. He saw the same threat to nature as to people. Machen, an avid hiker, saw in the wilderness of Maine the "wild exuberance of woods and streams gradually giving place to the dreary regularities of a National Park." Machen was hopeful, however, that the dissatisfaction with the modern world would lead people to seek Christ, the only source of freedom from "mechanism." [27] Fundamentalists did not develop probusiness or antibusiness groups; rather, individually they often had two minds about those methods, positive and critical, or they were just concerned about carrying the methods too far.

■

With the absorption of the emphasis on organization and efficiency, fundamentalists had merely accommodated to turn-of-the-century middle-class progressive ideals, but the consumer society, on a more massive scale by the 1920s, represented a new development for them and all of American society. Mass consumption in the 1920s further undermined the evangelical Protestant perspective that had prized hard work, self-discipline, and thrift. The social ethic shifted from production to consumption, prodded by sophisticated advertising in mass-circulation magazines and on the new medium, radio. Also, the taboo about debt had been broken for many Americans, and credit enabled them to consume even more. Before World War I houses were normally the only credit purchases people made, but after the war Americans increasingly purchased automobiles on the installment plan, and credit was democratized.[28]

Fundamentalists generally bought into at least the theory of consumerism in the 1920s with a vengeance by applying its principles to evangelism and church ministries. Historian Virginia Brereton has noted that especially by the 1920s Bible schools had a "flair for marketing and advertising." Fundamentalists at the time, as well as most Americans, did not sense the tension between an ethic of asceticism with an aversion to conspicuous consumption on the one hand and human impulsiveness bred by advertising on the other hand. Furthermore, they were not conscious of the changes in capitalism that generated the clash of values. A spiritual movement, blinded in part by the business success of the decade, swallowed materialist assumptions with ease.[29]

The implications are significant because social scientists argue that around the turn of the century Americans looked less to religion for happiness and more to large, efficient organizations that provided goods and services. The new morality valued a higher standard of living over a spiritual quest as the source of fulfillment. As some conservative evangelicals peddled religion like the newest mouthwash, implicitly its spiritual core was diminished. But they were not alone. Social gospelers also adapted to the consumer society, embracing its secular assumptions, treating religion as a product, and pursuing psychological well-being as a goal.[30]

Fundamentalists did not originate this flair for consumption, but they built on an evangelical affinity for it dating back to the eighteenth century. George Whitefield, star evangelist of the Great Awakening, according to one scholar, understood the economic changes in Great Britain and America and utilized mass-marketing techniques, specifically borrowed from the stage, to ply his trade. Dwight L. Moody, despite his resistance to secularization, his conservative social views, and his primary focus on the spiritual mission of redeeming souls, adapted to the consumer culture of the late nineteenth century in significant ways. To reach Chicagoans he used mobile circus-like tents for meetings, issued theater-like tickets for service, sadvertised with "Gospel Wagons," and improved communications with new technologies like voice recording.[31]

In the early 1900s some fundamentalists anticipated the hype and the intense promotionalism characteristic of the following decade. G. H. Meinardi met Bob Jones Sr. in 1914 at Winona Lake, a favorite Bible conference resort in Indiana, and joined his evangelistic team as business manager. A "high class" traveling salesman out of Chicago, according to one reporter, Meinardi had previously worked territory from Boston to Denver. What he had learned as a traveling salesman he used now in evangelistic work with Jones. Meinardi mixed well with all types of people, took the gospel to them, and still could be a "keen, 'hard-headed' business man and industrial hustler," "peddling the gospel of the cross with just as much earnest sincerity as he used to sell goods on the road." During the war one Baptist pastor proposed methods to keep people in church and out of the "picture show" on Sunday night: attractive sermon titles (for example, "Has the State University Become a Hot-bed of Heterodoxy?"), a 15-piece orchestra and 150-member youth choir, young men as ushers, and testimonies about how preferable church was to the movie house.[32]

Sinclair Lewis's *Elmer Gantry*, with its charlatan infidel, popularized a tawdry image of evangelists in the 1920s, an extreme model that missed the mark for most business-oriented religious workers. A valid message from *Elmer Gantry*, however, was the manner in which the techniques for the ministry and salesmanship had become interchangeable. An editor for the *Wheaton Record*, a student newspaper, noted that salespeople at sales conferences were motivated by calls not just for money but also for service and loyalty. Christians, the editor continued, should be motivated even more by loyalty and service. "We are in the 'pep meeting'—College" and the appeal is the gospel, "the greatest product on earth," concluded the editor. Even the scholarly Machen, at the founding of Westminster Seminary in 1929, was not above the consumer metaphor; in an age of specialization, Westminster's "product" would be "specialists in the Bible," not social science or even religion.[33]

No fundamentalist entity in the 1920s exemplified religion as consumption, either at the wholesale or retail levels, better than the "largest and richest" of Bible schools, Moody Bible Institute (MBI). In 1927 in downtown Chicago its "empire" included thirty-four buildings, valued at

$4.5 million, and its student body totaled about one thousand in each of the day and evening schools. Beyond the several city blocks, MBI reached eleven thousand students with twenty-eight correspondence courses, and its periodical, *Moody Monthly*, had twenty to thirty thousand subscribers. In addition, radio station WMBI and the Bible Institute Colportage Association promoted the gospel and the school over the airwaves and through the printed page. Bible teachers, evangelists, and fund-raisers in the Extension Department spread the message far beyond Chicago. In the decade of the corporation, MBI had an operation worthy of the envy of any businessperson.[34]

Still, MBI did not lose the human touch, despite the large bureaucracy. *Moody Monthly*'s editor in 1923, James M. Gray, praised a summer school course for pastors that emphasized "salesmanship applied to evangelism." The course, taught by a professor of salesmanship from Syracuse University, stressed that "the time had come to lay less emphasis on the wholesale, and more on the retail, method of winning the different types of people in each community." In the end, as Moody himself had practiced, individuals had to win individuals to Christ, Gray concluded, and lest the reader become too charmed by the psychology of salesmanship, soul winning was supernatural and involved the Holy Spirit. There were limits, therefore, to the modern methods, but the ideal for Gray was a combination of old and new: the man who has "the touch of God" and "gracious tact" to help someone with a spiritual need "possesses that which angels might envy." Gray sought for a balance in his equivocation about consumption.[35]

Women as well forged religious work with the consumer ethos. Emily H. Butterfield, a Detroit architect and Sunday school teacher of young women, confidently offered advice on "How a business woman would apply business sense to the business of teaching girls the Bible." To "sell" the New Testament to young women, a teacher had to use humor; appreciate beauty, whether in dress or "wandering brooks," as a "point of contact" with them; exhibit "pep," keeping up with the "modern girl" by knowing fads and being "up on athletics"; apply her faith to everyday home, school, or business; do the "unexpected" without being "affected and crude"; and, last, and for Butterfield it seemed least, prayer. For one salesgirl the blend of faith and commerce turned from figurative to literal. She complained in the *Sunday School Times* about rude customers in the department store where she worked and sought advice about a proper Christian response. The answer: be a witness for Christ to the person on the other side of the counter, "reflect the glorious light of Jesus Christ." [36]

The force that drove the consumer society to a greater intensity by the 1920s was more sophisticated advertising. Men such as Albert Lasker and Bruce Barton created a modern advertising style that not only informed but also persuaded. In 1920 the J. Walter Thompson agency hired John B. Watson, a pioneer behaviorist, and within a few years psychological research played a role in advertising. Aided by radio and mass-circulation magazines, ads used an emotional appeal, not just factual. Advertising itself in the process became a social influence on the level of, some would contend, church or school, creating a new set of values. Advertisers had to persuade Americans, born to believe in such cardinal virtues as work and thrift, that the good life came with material possessions and that craving them, impulsively buying them, was not a sin. While the Apostle Paul had admonished believers to be content with their worldly condition, admen earned a living convincing Americans of the opposite. Beset by urbanization, industrialization, bureaucracy, and a loss of control of their own selves, Americans in the early twentieth century were vulnerable to the message of happiness from Madison Avenue. [37]

Advertising not only shaped consumerism but also had links to the evangelical past. Nineteenth-century revivalists with their appeals to profess Christ helped sanctify choice: choosing Christ yielded emotional well-being. Similarly, happiness could result from selecting a product in the marketplace. In fact, modern advertising developed out of the unsavory patent medicine industry, with hustlers operating on the fringes of revivalism. To push the point further, Rodney Clapp has argued that advertising has led to a "deification of dissatisfaction," a mainspring for the consuming ethos. Advertisers have so venerated this urge to buy that, consequently, economic and material well-being have increasingly supplanted faith in God's providence as a key to personal happiness. [38]

Businessman Asa G. Candler symbolizes the connection between religion and advertising. The devout Methodist bought the formula for Coca-Cola in 1891 and touted its therapeutic qualities with religious fervor. Candler may have thought Coke was good for people, but it really was not the commodity—it was the business ethos that he was employing. Coke was one of the first products to be massively advertised, and in 1912 the Advertising Club of America cited it as the best-advertised commodity in the country. Sales meetings ended with the singing of "Onward, Christian Soldiers," and Candler's vision for worldwide marketing may have developed from his knowledge of national and international missions.[39] Promotion could work for religion and business.

Attracted by the power of advertising to evangelize and boost the church, most fundamentalists vigorously endorsed advertising as a technique, while some remained ambivalent about or resistant to the spiritual and social impact of this tool of mass persuasion. Advertising was the most popular business method adapted for promotion by the church. Although newspaper advertising was most prevalent, posters, billboards, placards, and cards, all touting religion, revealed that the church borrowed heavily from the commercial world. The fit between the two was a natural one in some ways. Fundamentalists intended to persuade with their rhetoric, to exhort members of an audience to respond to the gospel, and the folksy approach of an evangelist could be especially effective. By the 1920s, Bible conferences, magazines, books, radio, film, and Bible schools, in addition to revivals and churches, expanded the audience. If the purpose was to save souls, then for a lot of fundamentalists the means were sanctified.[40]

Fundamentalists in the 1920s did not originate this device of popular appeal. Dwight L. Moody had advertised in Chicago newspapers, in the announcements section in the "amusement columns," since he did preach in secular amusement centers. Protestant magazines, such as *Christian Herald,* viewed their readers as consumers and carried ads from banks, trust companies, and investment houses and for various products. J. Frank Norris held a successful revival in Kentucky in the summer of 1911 and, given the results, decided to be more aggressive. He started advertising his Sunday night sermon in a Ft. Worth newspaper, and the church was packed. Advertising a sensational product brought results, and he never relented. Evangelist M. B. Williams in 1916 advised fellow evangelists that building a tabernacle provided the best publicity, but it had to be supplemented with newspaper ads that should be changed frequently, two-color billboards and posters, ads in public transportation, and signs in windows of public places. In the South, Williams believed less publicity was needed; singing and preaching would attract significant attention. That same year fellow evangelist Biederwolf exhorted his peers to "Advertise much, and in every possible way." An announcement from the pulpit no longer sufficed, he argued, because the devil advertises for the natural man, and the church has something the natural man does not want.[41]

By the 1920s fundamentalists understood the value of advertising, whether it was William Jennings Bryan celebrating Florida real estate with the pitch that it had the best winter in the country, ignoring problems like racetrack gambling and smuggling of liquor, or a New York broker who applied it more directly by inserting gospel appeals in newspapers in about fifteen cities in nearby New Jersey. Bob Jones Sr. relied on advertising and publicity: "The business of the church is to take the message to the people. The day has passed when you can ring a church bell and expect a crowd." In so doing, Jones believed he was following the example of Jesus, Paul, Wesley, and Whitefield. Promotion proved important to evangelism and to his new college. Founded in 1927, Bob Jones College emphasized music and speech instruction because Jones thought it made students "good show-window material for the Lord Jesus Christ." Before World War I testimonials had a poor reputation, marred by hustlers of patent medicines, but in the years following the war, with successful use by admen for such products as Lux soap and for movies, the image changed. Jones used testimonials in advertising to promote the school. "Had I gone to another college I would probably have been a perfect modern flapper, for that was just the direction in which I was headed," student Marjorie Parker confessed.[42]

Moody Bible Institute considered advertising vital. J. Richard Olson, a Minneapolis editor addressing the student body, recounted a story about a visiting bishop from Norway, who, when asked about his greatest impression about America, replied, "Let me see. I think it was that what you call Bull Durham." Advertising worked for business; therefore, the church "should advertise to show its faith in itself and in its Founder and Head, the Lord Jesus Christ." The church should "use" the press, Olson continued, feeding it brief accounts covering the basic "three W's" of journalism because the "newspaper is the most insistent feature in our public life." James Gray, even more strongly, contended that in an age of propaganda, which he saw as assaults on our "consciousness" by advertisers, "People can be made to believe and to do anything if only it is advertised enough." But promoting the gospel lagged behind, he complained, and he wondered what could be done to make men and women mindful of God and conscious of the need for salvation. Gray suggested that believers fund an advertising campaign in trolley cars across the country, on billboards, in periodicals, and on radio. "It would do more for humanity than Ivory soap and Lipton's tea and the Camel," and he asked, "why are the children of this generation permitted to be wiser than the children of light?"[43]

Joseph A. Richards, advertising agency president, pictured the evangelical mission in stark commercial terms in churches and in religious magazines. Just as the brass serpent served as an Old Testament advertisement for Israel's remedy for snake bites, Richards felt that Christ served as "GOD'S GREAT ADVERTISEMENT" and remedy for sin. Continuing to see salvation as a product, Richards considered the brass serpent lifted by Moses as a "preliminary layout" for the "divine layout," Christ. Exercising faith in Christ, according to Richards, signified spending faith "on God and His plan of salvation." Richards also argued for "spiritual church advertising" to sell the "good," the gospel. First a church should survey the community to determine facts about the "market" around it. For Richards, the pastor is the "first assistant sales manager," the "sales manager" is the Holy Spirit, who uses "advertising methods to promote the spread of the gospel," and the "competitor" is Satan. Of course, Richards added that all church advertising should be scriptural and "prayed over."[44]

Other fundamentalists expressed ambivalence about advertising. Billy Sunday criticized the materialism of the commercial world, the immorality often mixed with it, and advertising that fostered it. He derided frivolous consumption by women, and in a May 1917 sermon he mocked men for "hiding behind and beneath stocks and bonds, dry goods, infidelity, whiskey, beer, love of ease." On the other hand, Sunday implicitly accepted the subtle message of advertisers that happiness and fulfillment were worthy goals, facilitated by consumption. Acknowledging that automobiles brought joy and that jewelry looked nice, Sunday had adapted to the "therapeutic culture," part of the emerging values of the consumer society. Likewise, J. Oliver Buswell could denounce billboards with photography that appealed to the sins of the flesh but at the same time advertise Wheaton College in thirteen periodicals to attract students and financial support. Form, for the fundamentalist, could be distinguished from content. Properly used, advertising was not only good, but wise.[45]

Curiously, advertisers did not fear most the "moral fundamentalists" who attacked ads as "offensive and spiritually degrading"; according to some in the industry they could be appeased or ignored. Secular critics, from liberal intellectuals to the consumer movement, proved stronger moral critics of advertising, deeming it coarse, wasteful, exploitative, excessively materialistic, and sometimes dishonest. Advertisers dismissed some criticism as simple antagonism to capitalism. They defended their trade as providing information for the consumer, promoting efficiency in the mass market, which meant overall savings, and assuring the public of the quality of national brands. Since advertisers had received little criticism from evangelicals, they sensed no urgent need to defend its morality or ethics; Madison Avenue had succeeded in placating them.[46]

Part of the advertising impulse among fundamentalists included a sophisticated sense of publicity and promotion. The literary output was enormous—articles, books, pamphlets—and was often accompanied by a photograph of the author. Thus secular writers were not the only ones with egos, seeking sometimes to present their ideas and themselves. Accused of being a "publicity hound," John Roach Straton, a former newspaperman, defended his extensive writings, published sermons, books, articles in *Forum, North American Review, McCalls,* and syndicated newspaper work, as merely responding to requests from editors. Besides, he believed newspapers were the best way to reach the masses. Evangelist Biederwolf credited part of his success to getting publicity by convincing newspapermen that real news was "forthcoming" from revival campaigns, writing material about the campaigns, and delivering it to the press. One religious promoter noted the good advertising value of children, because once they were involved in a campaign, they were the "best publicity agency that a campaign can have, for they talk about it everywhere." Another argued that to promote church growth, a pastor had to have a long-term program to sustain attention, much the same way that a merchant discovers a one-time sale does not work for the long run or that an advertiser knows that only consistent advertising works, not a single ad. Homer Rodeheaver, Billy Sunday's song leader, recognized that his association with Sunday had advertising value, which meant he matched his salary with the sales of song books and had four dollars of income from outside sources for every dollar paid to him by Sunday. A fellow pastor viewed J. C. Massee as "the greatest religious publicist in the country." Though not sensational, he "put on a remarkable good show" with dramatic preaching and good music. He cultivated the press and obtained front-page newspaper coverage, and he was one of the first ministers in New England to use radio. "He knows how to sell religion," his colleague added.[47]

Years before the hoopla of Dayton, Tennessee, and the Scopes Trial, William Jennings Bryan packed them in at his Tourist Bible Class in Miami, Florida. In the winter of 1917–18 Bryan had substituted for the Sunday school teacher, and his voice attracted tourists through the open doors and window; before the class ended the number grew to sixty listeners. The next week, with an even larger crowd, Bryan moved across the street to a park with a bandstand and benches. Eventually four to six thousand people frequented the "largest Bible class in the world," and by the early 1920s Bryan's Sunday school lessons were syndicated in about one hundred newspapers. Bryan was paid well for them, augmenting his income from real estate.[48]

Chicago-based evangelist Paul Rader understood promotion perhaps better than any other fundamentalist. Before stints as pastor of Moody Church, president of the Christian and Missionary Alliance, and pastor of Chicago Gospel Tabernacle, he started out as a street preacher in Pittsburgh. Though a fourth-generation minister, Rader had first experimented with the world as a football player, boxer, cowboy, bellhop, and coach before settling into the clerical life. His methods, "jazzing up" religion as he called it, drew criticism, but he also drew crowds. Four days a week during the late 1920s he held services in the LaSalle Theater in Chicago's Loop District. "Surrounded on every hand by theatrical scenery," Rader delivered a message after some "spirited gospel music." When people from the crowd would come forward for salvation, the curtain was dropped and the stage served as a "prayer room." He not only reached people conveniently as they came and went in the city, but by carrying the service over radio station WHT he connected with ordinary Americans in businesses, shops, factories, and on the farm. Rader had skillfully tapped into the techniques of mass culture.[49]

Rader's flair for the theatrical extended to imitating the farewells and arrivals of Hollywood stars. After a world missions tour for five months he planned to return to Chicago's Union Station on Christmas Day in 1929, speak to a radio audience, and then address the public in the depot, followed by a thousand-car caravan to the Chicago Gospel Tabernacle, where he would speak again. Rader learned the ploy from an expert, Aimee Semple McPherson. In 1926 he had "filled in" at the huge Angelus Temple in Los Angeles in her absence. Her departure at the railroad station, a service in which Rader participated, apparently impressed him. He noted that newspaper cameras and newsreel movie cameras recorded the event, and the next morning in all the newspapers he admired that picture of his "praying God speed to Mrs. McPherson." Despite his rapport with the charismatic and unconventional McPherson, Rader continued to be a major fundamentalist leader into the 1930s. Fittingly, after his death in 1938, funeral services were held at the Hollywood Presbyterian Church, and burial followed in Forest Lawn Cemetery. Rader joined those whose secular antics he had cleverly adapted to evangelism.[50]

Some fundamentalists understood intuitively the tension between the need to get the public's attention and the need to maintain a pristine image. One attendee at a conference on church publicity reported the advantages of a community survey, a good church bulletin, the radio, or putting up an electric sign, but cautioned "that publicity has a tendency to exaggerate the ego and that there is need to be careful lest he be snared by a desire for personal advertising." Often the fundamentalist leader had to create a crisis to capture and sustain attention. Biederwolf, in 1915, advised ministers to be more like evangelists whose techniques worked, not because of crowds, appeals to human nature, or "the unusual and extraordinary," but due to preaching the gospel, which for Biederwolf meant exposing cults like Christian Science and Jehovah's Witnesses and liberals he termed "theological crawfish." One reporter noted that Biederwolf had succeeded in a Long Beach campaign where he attacked Christian Scientists and others, stirring strife in the community. The evangelist, it seemed to him, had to condemn the city where he presently preached as wicked, the worst city, for its crime and sin.[51] For Biederwolf, his gospel preaching and condemnation of the host city was "promotion" enough, for it clearly stirred controversy and attracted attention.

But Biederwolf knew that the evangelist could go too far, that some could be placed in the category of "the incompetent, the irresponsible and the erratic" and were guilty of "gross commercialism and extravagant sensationalism." He urged fellow evangelists to follow standards set by the Commission on Evangelism set up by the Federal Council of Churches. One provision called for a committee of pastors for an evangelistic campaign to guard against "inflated" results and "sensational advertising." Curtis Lee Laws worried that "unattractive" suburban Baptist churches, with people objecting to "humble surroundings, the poor music, the small congregation, and the preacher," were losing members, especially the wealthy and educated young people, to more fashionable churches such as Congregational ones. For him this image problem could be alleviated if suburban Baptist churches with "superior advantages" would help those "less wealthy or less cultured." On this point promotion intersected with class for this religious leader. Bob Jones Sr., also with a keen eye for appearance, insisted on educational standardization for his college, founded in 1927. To build his fledgling school he cooperated with public educators. He refused to join Buswell of Wheaton in a fight against educational standardization. At that point Jones focused more on creating academic quality, or at least the appearance of it, while other fundamentalist leaders feared conformity with outside standards.[52]

The founding of Bob Jones College in 1927, one of the most innovative fundamentalist promotions of the era, blended business with Christian education. At the height of his evangelistic career, Jones switched to an academic pursuit, building a school where modernist and secular threats would not destroy the faith of young people. In early 1926, before the September hurricane wrecked the real estate boom in Florida, Jones had already selected a site near Lynn Haven, Florida, eight miles from Panama City and near his southern Alabama birthplace. R. L. MacKenzie, a Panama City promoter and real estate agent, and Bibb Graves of Alabama persuaded him to come to that area, and MacKenzie helped devise a development whereby the college would be built in the midst of a new community. A promotional brochure touted the project "In Florida's Indian Summerland on Beautiful St. Andrews Bay" as a culminating ambition of

Bob Jones. The evangelist envisioned a combination of Northfield, Massachusetts, Winona Lake, Indiana, and Chautauqua, New York, going beyond the Bible conference to provide "the greatest Christian scholars, and teachers in the world there." Jones's real estate venture had a precedent. In the early 1890s Dwight L. Moody and benefactor Turlington Harvey built an ideal Christian community, Harvey, Illinois, but self-government in a few years brought an end to the "utopia," an echo of the communitarian settlements of the 1830s and 1840s.[53]

Minor C. Keith Properties, Inc., handled the 2,500-acre development for Jones, selling lots for $1,000 to $2,000, with 25 percent of the income designated for the construction and operation of the college, and donated 470 acres for the campus. Jones, instead of gifts, solicited buyers for lots in the subdivision to "help us build this great college." "We have made an arrangement by which a man can make a safe and . . . profitable investment and at the same time do our college as much good as if they gave the money outright," he declared in a letter to friends. Despite the depressed real estate market after the September 1926 hurricane, Jones and the board of trustees issued $500,000 in bonds to build the first unit of college buildings. In the second year of the school the board sold $25,000 in additional bonds. Jones challenged supporters to invest money that will "work for you and at the same time it will work for the Lord." During the Great Depression this unusual financial structure would become untenable.[54]

A common feature of what historian Virginia Brereton called "the selling-the-gospel approach" of fundamentalists was the widespread use of periodicals. In addition to the major ones—*Moody Monthly, Sunday School Times* and *King's Business*—most fundamentalist leaders or institutions boasted one. In 1926 J. Frank Norris shot an unarmed man three times and unrepentantly used the incident to increase the circulation of his magazine, the *Searchlight,* changed a year later to the *Fundamentalist.* Bob Shuler in 1922 started publishing *Bob Shuler's Magazine,* financed by a longtime friend, and at its height it attracted twenty thousand paid subscribers in addition to newsstand sales. William Bell Riley's *Pilot,* along with his books, helped fulfill his belief that the "printed page has power" that is more influential than radio. Bob Jones in June 1928 introduced his *Bob Jones Magazine* not as an organ of the college but as a "way of communicating with my friends."[55]

Those who edited and published the periodicals employed rather sophisticated marketing savvy. Beginning with its September 1920 issue, the *Christian Workers Magazine* became the *Moody Bible Institute Monthly.* The word *Moody* had appeared in a previous incarnation of the magazine's title, and management thought it wise to bring it back, most likely because of its name identification. Furthermore, at the same time the Moody periodical changed its shape to a larger format to correspond to the *Literary Digest,* which was the standard periodical form for the time and which allowed more print, larger type, more illustrations, and greater economy for advertising. Three years later the *King's Business* switched as well to the popular larger format. Advertising in *Moody Monthly* featured health aids, novel inventions, small businesses, and Montgomery Ward, but most ads offered Christian literature or ministry aids such as hymn books, choir robes, and portable organs. In 1935 Will Houghton replaced long-time editor James M. Gray. The name changed to *Moody Monthly,* and the magazine shifted from serious commentary, which had emphasized fundamentalist topics such as dispensational premillennialism as well as political and social issues, to more traditional, devotional ones. Paid circulation had doubled from 20,000 in 1921 to 40,000 in 1935. This fundamentalist periodical, an aid to laypeople and a magazine for MBI alumni, provided reports from graduates, ministry tips, testimonies, Bible studies, and theological, political, and social commentary. The formula sold, and *Moody Monthly, King's Business,* and *Sunday School Times* were the mainstream fundamentalist periodicals.[56]

Radio, with its advertising, also fueled the consumer society of the 1920s and contributed significantly to the commodification of religion. On January 2, 1921, KDKA in Pittsburgh broadcast from Calvary Episcopal Church and ushered in religious radio programming; by 1925 seventy-one churches or religious organizations had licenses. As historian Martin Marty has observed, conservatives exploited this technology more effectively than the liberal Protestants. Straton's Calvary Baptist Church was the first to broadcast regularly in New York City. BIOLA had its own station, KJS, in 1922, and Moody Bible Institute followed four years later with WMBI. Just as evangelists Moody and Sunday had embraced new technologies, fundamentalists in the 1920s quickly appreciated the potential for radio. Not only could they reach more people with the gospel through radio, but they could build constituencies, merge the religious appeal with mass culture, and even build a foundation for greater cultural authority.[57]

Radio as a form of promotion did pose some questions for believers. T. C. Horton of the *King's Business* shared mixed feelings over this "newest agency for broadcasting the gospel," which he also saw as "another menace to the spread of the gospel." The devil was, after all, "the prince of the power of the air," and the objections were serious: radio was expensive; it could engender a "stay-at-home" attitude and hurt the offerings; would it persuade as well as the preacher, live, in person, in the pulpit; and would it lead to conversions to Christ? Despite his being "restless over the radio," Horton concluded that the church should use the medium of radio "to advertise the Gospel." Moody officials also cautioned Christians over the coming years about the new technology. Just as with the automobile, the phonograph, and the motion picture, scientific progress brought problems. Most programming was secular, so the believer had to exercise care in using radio. The greater audience potential for radio evangelism was offset somewhat by the casual radio listeners. Christian broadcasters had to "avoid cheapness": "a radio program is worth all the study and labor and skill which can be put into it."[58]

Others praised the new device unambiguously. Mrs. Bob Jones Sr., reflecting her husband's sentiments at the opening of a radio station, considered "a modern radio station about the most democratic institution in our modern life" since it allowed programs for all groups. Bryan termed it the "greatest invention placed to the credit of human intelligence." In a radio address from a church in 1922 over Pittsburgh's KDKA, Bryan suggested that "to hurl my words through space" pointed to a moral lesson, "that the spiritual world surrounds us." Only those with receivers can hear over the air, and, Bryan added, only those "in tune with the Infinite" can receive spiritual insights. Charles G. Trumbull, convinced of the effectiveness of the radio for evangelism, challenged Christians to follow Christ's command to make friends of the "mammon of unrighteousness," conceding its relation to the evil of the present age.[59]

Paul Rader illustrates the aggressiveness with which fundamentalists adapted radio to evangelism. On June 15, 1922, the mayor of Chicago invited Rader and his musicians to his station, WHT, to fill up program time. Rader broadcast from the crude shack on the roof of city hall that served as the studio, and his fame spread. Two days later the *Chicago*

Daily News carried a story about the "enterprising preacher," and listeners phoned in. Within three years Rader had organized *The National Radio Chapel* program, "conducting its services every Sunday in a vast ethereal cathedral." "Pews" were everywhere there were radios, and his "pulpits" were the studio of his Chicago Gospel Tabernacle and the studio of WHT. The *National Radio Chapel Announcer* magazine listed "Radio Relatives," financial backers of the radio ministry. Programs from noon to 11:30 P.M. on Sunday included not only preaching and music but also targeted young boys and girls, young women, shut-ins, and missions. In 1926 Rader renamed his magazine the *World-Wide Christian Courier* and attracted people without radios who lived overseas. Rader estimated that in 1928 fifty million people had listened to his Sunday radio broadcasts. In April 1930 he announced a "chain hook-up" with CBS, adding ten key stations in central and eastern states, for a total listening audience of 70 million people. A "Breakfast Brigade" of morning listeners would support the effort financially. Rader's folksy, informal, Will Rogers–like style and his natural, soft-spoken radio voice, peppered with occasional dramatic intensity, gave him mass appeal.[60]

To his critics who deplored this "tool of the devil," Rader retorted that the church had to go to the world, for the world would not come to it. For those worried about hurting attendance, Rader argued that radio could adversely affect liberal churches but would increase attendance at "New Testament" ones through converts. For him, radio was the "Greatest Evangel." Rader's radio director and announcer, Floyd B. Johnson, believed the evangelistic opportunities were "unprecedented" but felt quality programming required hard work, ingenuity, and prayer. "Broadcasting without Prayer is only Entertainment" read a sign on the church's studio wall. A business executive friend of Rader's pointed out that radio was good for the city: "there is something else in life besides the struggles of business . . . that will make . . . hearts lighter . . . work more cheerful and . . . homes brighter." In addition to evangelism, technology, and business, Rader's efforts resonated with premillennialism. Rader described President Coolidge, whose inaugural address was delivered on radio, as the first announcer of a universal message and stated that with Christ's Second Coming, "There will be another ANNOUNCER on the air before long."[61]

Others quickly sensed the effectiveness of radio for promotion and evangelism. In 1922, the same year Rader ventured into broadcasting, BIOLA's KJS broadcast from Los Angeles to places five hundred to three thousand miles away—Hartford, Connecticut, and Henderson, Alabama. The following year, greater wattage allowed the signal to reach South and Central America, Mexico, Canada, and all parts of the United States. Instead of an audience of three to four thousand in the school's Church of the Open Door auditorium, R. A. Torrey could speak over radio from the pulpit to an estimated one hundred thousand people.[62]

In 1925 Moody Bible Institute accepted an invitation from WGES in Chicago for two of their student cornetists to play on the air. An offer of free air time followed for Sundays, and the endeavor proved so successful the school purchased time from that station and a second one. In 1926 MBI began broadcasting on its own station, WMBI. A few years later a school official recognized that the radio had united families around programs and personalities: "It is the modern altar erected in the center of the life of the world. It speaks with a voice of authority." Governments used radio for propaganda and business used it to advertise, he noted, and Christians could also tap into the "romance of the radio."[63]

In October 1926 Lizzie H. Glide, a wealthy benefactor, donated $25,000 to Bob Shuler to build a radio station. On December 26, 1926, he began broadcasting from the station built at his Trinity Methodist Church in Los Angeles. Attracting a constituency beyond his pulpit and magazine, Shuler could now compete with his Los Angeles rival, Aimee Semple McPherson, who had her own talents at self-promotion as a popular female evangelist. His KGEF reached an estimated 100,000 people in the West, Texas, the eastern states, and Canada. His good friend Bob Jones Sr. also shifted to radio for promoting his college. Three years after founding the school, Jones boasted that "no other institution in America is as widely represented by radio as is Bob Jones College." He told the story of the college every day over five stations in three states, claiming to reach a million listeners. E. Howard Cadle, Indianapolis evangelist and entrepreneur, utilized radio in an unusual way to expand his ministry, Cable Tabernacle, built in 1921. In the 1930s, after preaching over WLW, a Cincinnati station that covered the Midwest and much of the southern half of the United States, Cadle purchased hundreds of radios and distributed them to rural congregations with no full-time pastors. Those listeners became part of

his financial base. Cadle had learned from his prior business ventures—
auto sales, work for the National Biscuit Company, and a group of shoe
repair stores. With such emphasis on the use of radio, along with the increasing popularity of air travel, Stewart P. MacLennan, pastor of First
Presbyterian Church in Hollywood, anticipated with more certainty the
end of the age. Such "Universal Air-Mindedness" was a sign, he argued,
that Christ was soon coming in the air. Premillennialism and the business
ethos, revealed in a zealous use of radio promotion, coexisted with little
difficulty for many fundamentalists.[64]

Periodicals and radio spread the gospel message but also promoted the
messenger in ways that accentuated another aspect of the commercial
spirit of the 1920s, a focus on expansion and numbers. Fundamentalist
enterprises grew steadily throughout the decade, despite the 1925 Scopes
Trial and the attendant bad publicity. Bible colleges flourished between
World War I and 1930, with seventeen new ones founded during this age
of expansion. Leaders attracted students and funds through periodicals
and radio and further emphasized education through book publishing,
Bible conferences, and film. Fundamentalist liberal arts colleges thrived.
Wheaton College went from 240 students in 1922 to 456 in 1927, almost doubling its enrollment. In 1922 President Charles A. Blanchard of
Wheaton envisioned greater growth: "within ten years a Christian university: faculties of arts, theology, law, medicine, and technology, with
ten thousand students; every faculty manned by avowed Christian men."
Blanchard hoped "some Christian businessman" would organize "that
great machine" of Christian higher education. Two years after its founding in 1927, Bob Jones College had over 200 students from eleven states.
Bob Jones Sr. still held revival meetings, advertised in several religious
periodicals, and had a good mailing list, all of which attracted students.
The Association of Business Men's Evangelistic Clubs, organized in 1921
in Atlanta with 17 clubs from six states, had expanded to 131 clubs in
nine states by 1929. This interdenominational group of business laymen
engaged in various evangelistic activities in coordination with local
churches.[65] An emphasis on results, not merely a focus on the spiritual, revealed how strongly business methods had affected fundamentalists. There
would also be more graphic indications of that influence in the 1920s.

2 Reflecting on the Consumer Society

Fundamentalists appropriated the business ethos in the 1920s, with its emphases on organization, efficiency, consumption, promotion, advertising, and growth, so pervasively that when Bruce Barton published his *The Man Nobody Knows,* the best-selling nonfiction book in the country for 1925 and 1926, they reacted with remarkably little protest. Barton, a minister's son, a prominent Republican, and an advertising executive, remade Christ to fit the image of modern business, the salesman as hero of the 1920s. Countering an old Sunday school image of Christ as weak, Barton depicted him as a "muscular Christian," "the most popular dinner guest in Jerusalem," and a leader, "the founder of modern business." "He picked up twelve men from the bottom ranks of business and forged them into an organization that conquered the world." Christ was a consumer, turning water into wine, and "The parable of the Good Samaritan is the greatest advertisement of all time." On the flyleaf of the book Barton focused the reader on the key to his analysis with a passage from Luke 2:49, Christ's response to his parents: "Wist ye not that I must be about my Father's *business?*" [1]

The book had an unmistakably modernist tone. "Let us forget all creed for the time being, and take the story just as the simple narratives give it," Barton stated early in the text. "Overemphasizing the human side of his character," Barton consciously sought to offset the overemphasis others had placed on Christ's deity. "Son of man" was Christ's favorite title for himself, Barton declared. His Christ was all too human. Jesus was "less the prophet, more and more the companion." Mirroring the 1920s therapeutic culture, Barton further added: "This was his message—a happy God, wanting His sons and daughters to be happy." Jesus would be comfortable with Babbitry. According to Barton, Christianity conquered, not due to demand, but because Jesus and his disciples knew how to sell it. He had the techniques of "modern salesmanship": anticipating and meeting objections and the use of a single question in persuasion. Christ "would be a national advertiser today." Consistent with Barton's common portrait, the book closes with Christ's death, not resurrection.[2]

Other elements could have troubled fundamentalists. Barton challenged man's sinfulness, Christ's atonement for sin, and the harmony of the gospels. Barton's god was not the fundamentalist God: "a great Companion, a wonderful Friend, a kindly indulgent, joy-loving Father." He was not a "petulant Creator," "not a stern Judge."[3]

General fundamentalist silence about this modernist portrait of Christ proved puzzling to Barton, who intended to provoke them. Barton pressed his publisher to get John Roach Straton to "roast" the book. He objected to a Gothic window being used in advertising the book: "I don't like the window frame because it suggests the very ecclesiastical atmosphere against which the book is a protest." Barton, also expecting protests from Catholics, was disappointed when the amount was less than anticipated. He wanted to shock but did not want to alienate the public by appearing irreverent. "The word 'reverent' should be used in every piece of copy," he advised his publisher. Years later he confided that, concerned about the potential irreverence of the book, he sent the manuscript to his mother, "a saint of the old school," to read and that if she thought it irreverent, he "would burn it up and forget it." After her approval he pursued publication. Still, Charles Scribner's Sons rejected the book, fearing it would "be a shock" to the general public because of the "impression of an apparent irreverence." In its review the New York Times underscored the dilemma: "Mr. Barton's interpretation is certain to shock many readers, though it is reverent."[4]

In several ways Barton's book disarmed fundamentalist critics even as he intended to antagonize them. Historian Frederick Lewis Allen observed that "the association of business with religion was one of the most significant phenomena of the day." There were precedents for Barton's message. Russell Conwell, a Baptist minister who died in 1925, preached the sermon "Acres of Diamonds" over six thousand times, telling Chautauqua audiences that making money was equal to the heart of the gospel. Popular in the early 1920s with two books on religion and business, writer and Congregationalist Roger Babson sounded like Max Weber with an emphasis on such values as hard work, thrift, honesty, and efficiency. Richard Hofstadter has argued that Billy Sunday's "new violence of expression," typical of clergy during the World War I era, paved the way for the coarseness, or poor taste for some, of Barton's prose. Barton took the business ethos a step further. Historian Warren I. Susman has argued that *The Man Nobody Knows* was a "means of sanctifying the new order of modern business," not just justifying capitalism and its virtues. Others have noted that Barton blended the worlds of business and religion, diminishing faith to fit the business creed of the 1920s and debasing Christ as a businessman but elevating businessmen to be "ministers" of Christ. The celebration of business as a national religion reassured businesspeople that their behavior was in line with traditional religion. This embrace of religion, superficial though it was, was difficult for conservative Protestants, already enamored of business, to attack.[5]

What the *New York Times* referred to as Barton's "Rotarian vision" perhaps tugged at fundamentalist hearts and made attacks upon it awkward. Business clubs like Kiwanis and Rotary mushroomed in the 1920s, and by promoting moral codes and spiritual ideals of business and offering sources of fellowship, they often supplanted the functions of Protestant churches. When Barton talked about service, self-reliance, humility, and going the second mile, it sounded like the gospel of some churches, even though it contradicted evangelical Christianity with its stress on humans and social conditions. Again the effort by Barton to make the secular "divine" likely left some fundamentalists too nonplussed to criticize, especially since he was attacking selfishness.[6]

Furthermore, fundamentalists could not argue very much with a book critical of liberal Protestantism. Countering the soft, weak, effeminate Christ, possibly of his father's modernist faith, Barton promoted a more physical and masculine Savior, an outdoorsman, manual laborer, and a man who enjoyed the company of men. These manly features reverberated with the go-getter creed of the 1920s salesman and, importantly, also with fundamentalist efforts to counter feminine influence in American society, especially in the churches, during the era of the new woman. Years earlier Barton revealed that he shared this "muscular" Christianity when he wrote a favorable article on Billy Sunday. To Barton, Sunday embodied "energy and virility"; fundamentalists could only say "amen."[7]

Barton represented a far more subtle transition that fundamentalists and others did not fully perceive. *The Man Nobody Knows* shows a Barton torn between the old work-ethic values, concerns about character, and the emerging "therapeutic culture" in which a sense of well-being derived, not from morality, but from physical and emotional health. Orthodox Protestants had emphasized diligence, human sinfulness, and the need for salvation and had decried indulgence and idleness. Barton's creed turned all that on its head. Leisure and consumption were vital in the search for happiness and fulfillment. To him, Christ had a great personality and was a socializer, an inspirer, the epitome of the 1920s salesman. *The Man Nobody Knows* was not a Christian book but a success manual for businessmen, yet in his spiritualizing about the corporation, Barton furnished his reader with a "theology" for a secular age and by mixing advertising and therapeutic ideals with religion kept potential critics off balance. To fundamentalists, faith was very special, but they also adored capitalism and could not easily complain when Barton celebrated the two in, what seemed to many, an innocent fashion.[8]

Barton and fundamentalists shared an enthusiasm for persuasion, one promoting consumer products, the other urging people to become Christians. "Advertising, then, was persuasion and persuasion could and would change the world," Barton believed, in the judgment of Warren I. Susman. Paul Rader in a sermon titled "Who Put the Ad in Advertising?" concluded that God did. Ad writers, he argued, could not do better than John 3:16, the greatest advertisement ever read. "God is the leading advertiser," he continued. "He has written His ads in every rock." Little wonder that Paul Maynard in the advertising department of the *Christian Herald* expressed "delight" in Barton's book and purchased five copies to give to friends. A few weeks later, in January 1927, his magazine featured an illustration of a businessman facing a factory, bond papers in hand, with the caption: "The American businessman—the hero of the age."[9]

Other positive comments revealed an affinity for Barton's emphasis. Reverend Robert Clark, writing in the *Moody Monthly*, acknowledged questions about the accuracy of Barton's picture of Christ but reasoned: "At any rate he drew the attention of a large number of people to the person of Christ, and in that we rejoice." Charles W. Koller, a Newark, New Jersey, Baptist pastor, considered Barton more liberal than himself but could "sincerely rejoice in the success" of his later work, *The Book Nobody Knows.* "I believe it will do much to bring the Bible to the favorable attention of such as have not become familiar with its blessed contents," he speculated. Edward W. Grilley Jr., a twenty-one-year-old student at Moody's Mt. Hermon School, described Barton's books as "inspired, sensible, manly, sincere pictures of the Gospels and of Christ Jesus." *The Man Nobody Knows,* "a wonderful book," was especially praised: "This wish-washy, [*sic*] effeminate Christ must be shut out of Christendom—and it is only done . . . by such candid, inspired works as those of the Bruce Barton type." Barton's editor predicted that the "world's best Babbitt" could be persuaded to read his book and afterward would "be as strong for Jesus as he now is for his local Rotary." The reverse happened for a Kansas pastor, who inquired of the *Sunday School Times* if he could join the Rotary Club without violating scriptural injunctions about being "unequally yoked together with unbelievers." The editor responded that joining the Rotary would not be contrary to scripture, pointing out it was a service organization, not religious, and not a secret order.[10]

Other factors help explain fundamentalists' tacit assent to Barton's message. Laurence R. Iannaccone has pointed out that fundamentalists in the late twentieth century paid little attention to economic questions; in fact, "there is no generally accepted biblical standard for economic conduct." While rank and file are supportive of capitalism, fundamentalist and evangelical leaders reveal a wide variety of thought, from free market to even socialism, for some left-wing evangelicals. Perhaps fundamentalist economic views are not exceptional; like other Americans they "adapt it to their own purposes," depending on the secular circumstances. As with technology, he concluded that "Fundamentalists appear to appropriate economic concepts in much the same way: picking and choosing, paying little attention to an item's original source, and above all use everything they can as an instrument to further their religious . . . agenda." That economic flexibility, true as well for the 1920s, allowed fundamentalists to embrace, pragmatically, Barton's book. On a more practical level, the Christian response to Barton may have mirrored their mixed feelings about the turn-of-the-century commercialization of Christmas. Although they may have been disillusioned by it, they were delighted that the holiday had been elevated in the culture. Christmas, like Barton's Christ, had been both "secularized" and "sacralized." [11]

The few fundamentalists who attacked Barton focused on theological and spiritual differences, not business philosophy. William Jennings Bryan, a few months before the Scopes Trial and his death, admitted to Barton's publisher that the book was an "unusual mixture of things praiseworthy and objectionable" but protested that it discredited the supernatural aspects of Christ. Barton, a modernist according to Bryan, denied orthodox tenets like the virgin birth and the Resurrection. Furthermore, Bryan resented the presumption of the title, implying that Jesus was not known until Barton discovered him. The old progressive did not object, apparently, to Barton's marriage of Christ and Bryan's old enemy, business. In fact, Bryan by this point in his life was something of a business enthusiast himself. Arno Gaebelein, in a response to Barton, charged that the book "stabs . . . at the very heart of Christianity" and described Barton's ideas as "perversions." "Can the conception of Christ as a business man . . . give our conscience rest and bring us nigh unto God? No! Nothing but the blood of Jesus," Gaebelein declared. The *Sunday School Times* attacked Barton for challenging the historicity of Daniel as well as the claims of Christ and the Bible. The *Moody Monthly* ran a devotion on "The Man I Know," a mild spiritual critique based on Paul's declaration to Timothy, "for I know him whom I have believed." [12]

One critic, however, ventured beyond just a spiritual assault on Barton and dared question the business ethos. Amos H. Gottschall, in a booklet published by himself, denounced Barton as a "modernist of a rank type" and excoriated the "prodigious audacity" and "sacrilegious stabbing" of the work, but he also argued that Barton's central point was fallacious. "His mission was not money making," Gottschall declared. "He did not leave Heaven and come to earth in order to teach men the tricks of trade, or how to promote commercial enterprises." Later Gottschall proclaimed, "How sacrilegious to drag things sacred and divine down to the level of the sordid and mercenary of earth." Christ came "to save a lost race . . .

not to fit people for modern business life, but citizenship in Heaven," Gottschall reasoned.[13]

Despite these criticisms, fundamentalists remained generally quiet about Barton's book, remarkable given their aggressiveness on other fronts during those years and also noteworthy because the few others who disagreed with Barton did speak out. Catholic readers took offense with his attack on the virginity of Mary and the assertion that Catholics worshiped Mary. Some liberal Protestants spoke out against Barton and the materialism of the 1920s. Even one self-described lapsed Methodist, who had rejected the orthodoxy of her childhood, resented more vehemently than most fundamentalists Barton's efforts: "[his] articles, to my mind, have the effect of bringing Christ from the ineffable to the commonplace. Same thing as using the American flag on a hokey pokey ice cream cart. . . . Mr. Barton discusses Him as casually as he would a candidate for Sheriff. This is the age of jazz; let us keep Christ's mystery inviolable."[14]

The muted response to Barton's *The Man Nobody Knows* appears more enigmatic in view of some general criticisms of business by fundamentalists before and during the 1920s. Those misgivings, along with their enthusiastic embrace of the commercial spirit, revealed a thorough ambivalence toward business. In the Progressive Era, attacks on big business were not unusual. A trust that sought to destroy a competitor, according to A. C. Dixon, was a "devil-fish whose slimy tentacles should be cut off by law." Furthermore, he warned that "all ministers should keep themselves untrammeled by money-making schemes." William Bell Riley decried the "universal prevalence of a commercial spirit which casts all conscience aside," "growing and grasping corporations," and businesspeople with "methods of piling up millions, escaping taxes, buying up legislative bodies, bullying voters, and oppressing" workers. Later he charged that corporate wealth was too closely tied to the church. James M. Gray linked commerce, the trust, and end times, calling commercialism the "first-born daughter of Babylon." International business, Gray predicted, would create the "greatest trust," the revival of the old Roman Empire, all preparation for the Antichrist. Business "has filled the world with its numerous forms of wickedness," with Sabbath violations, evil amusements, and corruption of politics. On the eve of World War I, Bob Jones Sr., during a crusade in the New York area sponsored by Moody Bible Institute, declared that with "hellfire and damnation" preaching, "Rich malefactors would cease defying the government."[15]

A thread of the Progressive critique of capitalism persisted in the 1920s among some fundamentalists, even those who had embraced the decade's business spirit. They occasionally cited spiritual deficiencies, connected some businesses, especially the trusts, to vices, chided both business and labor, and sometimes defended the latter. The central issue for many fundamentalists was not the capitalist system but the morality of the individual businessman. Paul Rader, quoting Roger W. Babson, as fundamentalists often did, challenged businessmen not to lose "high spiritual ideals in the scramble for material things." Rader saw his spiritual work in Chicago as the "salt" that retards "human rottenness that causes panics." At the close of the decade, L. R. Akers, president of Asbury College, warned students at Bob Jones College in chapel that America's greatest peril was the "worship of material success." This "love of gold," measuring achievement in terms of wealth, a "material miasma," permeated American society, he asserted.[16]

Big business was a special target for sometimes stressing profit and efficiency over morals. John Roach Straton contended that evil was "organized and exploited in a large business way" in that "modern vice is . . . commercialized." For some fundamentalist ministers the offense extended beyond the immorality of movies, theater, and liquor. J. C. Massee criticized businessmen for a host of sins in the 1920s: putting mammon before God and family, operating sweatshops "where children are done to death," running tenements that force "together human beings as cattle under conditions which promote sickness, disease and death," and hurting the public by bribing inspectors, selling fraudulent stock, and restraining trade. William Bell Riley ascribed the ultimate evil to one big businessman; he attacked the Rockefeller trust as Antichrist for introducing liberalism into Protestantism through his endowment of the University of Chicago.[17]

Often these conservative Protestants chastised both capital and labor. In his popular lecture-sermon during the 1920s, "Perils of America," Bob Jones Sr. sounded the alarm about "extreme wealth and extreme poverty." The accumulation of wealth in this country by men like Henry Ford and the power of labor unions were both inevitable parts of American life, he concluded. The solution was to "Christianize" both, not just the workers but also "the men who control the wealth in this country." Straton railed against "unjust wages, especially to women workers, child labor, the hell-black social evil, lawlessness, and the . . . liquor traffic." "Christ came to disturb bad business conditions," he continued, and today ministers needed to drive the "money changers from the temple of modern civilization!" Labor had a "wrong spirit"—"anarchists," he called them once—whereas businessmen, also selfish, were termed "millionaire highwaymen." R. A. Torrey suspected that poverty would continue due to laziness on one side and greed on the other; only Christ's return would cure the ills of the urban poor and business.[18]

Implicit in the occasional harsh words for business was a sympathy for working-class Americans. "I see the human hogs that dominate so much of the business and politics and society of our day," Torrey wistfully observed, "and trample the weak under their feet . . . those who are underneath in the present mad scramble that we call business." Straton identified himself as an "outspoken friend and champion" of working people, sympathetic for their rights and a better standard of living. Motives other than humanitarian sometimes drove their concern: some linked low wages for women as a cause for prostitution and felt labor abuses would enhance the appeal of communism among workers. Such sentiments harked back to an earlier age, prior to the 1920s, when conservative evangelicals showed greater social concerns.[19]

Some conservative Christians disapproved of advertising, at least its excesses and misrepresentations. L. R. Akers complained that advertisements in modern magazines idolized materialism and defined success in terms of wealth, not spiritual values. Massee noted the hypocrisy of merchants with stores closed on Sunday advertising heavily in Sunday newspapers and people on Sunday who "regale their minds with prospective bargains." The *Sunday School Times* felt compelled apparently to respond to a letter to the editor critical of the periodical, "a spiritual paper," for carrying any advertising at all. Charles G. Trumbell defended advertising in the magazine as an "important part of its spiritual ministry to its readers" and as financially necessary for covering publishing costs.[20]

Anecdotal evidence suggests that some fundamentalist women rejected the commercial spirit of the 1920s. In the pages of the *Sunday School*

Times a "farm mother" complained to her college son about the business impulse: "I feel on entering a department [in a dime store] as if I were about to be operated on." Relieved that her son had not been "very seriously bitten" by the commercial spirit, she continued, "I am sorry that the demands of an industrial age are compelling us to learn the tricks of the trade." But even this mother revealed later in the article her ambiguous feelings about enterprise: "Everyone of us who has any serious convictions has something to sell," and her son's friend who had sold Fuller brushes "ought to be a better preacher for the things he learned at those salesmen pep meetings."[21] Even among the doubters, the conventions of business held firm.

Some women undoubtedly experienced the dilemma that H. L. Mencken described for members of the Kiwanis: "they have not discovered how to make life amusing. Worse, they have not discovered how to make it important." In 1923 the *Sunday School Times* initiated an advice column for girls, responding to problems they might encounter as modern Christian women, including those in the business world. One young girl wrote to "Mother Ruth," despairing of the business world as a "treadmill" and sensing her worth only in commercial terms. The columnist advised that if spiritual values had priority in her life then her commercial world would be a "delight."[22]

During the 1930s fundamentalists viewed capitalism far more critically than they had in the previous decade, again exhibiting mixed feelings about it. The Great Crash and the deepening depression did more than scriptural admonitions had done to sour them on the excesses of the business civilization. As prosperity ebbed, concerns over finances mounted, in some cases replacing disquietude over evolution and modern theology. Ivan J. Fahs, though converted during Mordecai Ham's Charlotte, North Carolina, revival campaign in 1934, complained that the evangelist's "constant harranging [sic] of the audience for money" took up a large part of the meeting and was "undignified." Fundamentalists had reason to worry: many ministries faltered financially. In 1933 the Chicago Gospel Tabernacle went into receivership. *Bob Shuler's Magazine,* with a 75 percent decrease in subscribers, ceased publication in July 1933. Shuler had started the periodical in 1922 but due to the depression could not maintain its previously strong subscription list and newsstand sales.[23]

Bob Jones Sr. encountered severe financial problems. In 1931 he ceased publishing his magazine and switched to radio. Each issue of the magazine had cost about $300 to print, and "in these hard times we can spend the money more advantageously by giving the gospel over the radio," he shared with his readers. Before the depression his revival campaigns generated between fifty thousand and seventy-five thousand dollars a year for the college; during the depression it dipped to five to seven thousand dollars a year. Students sometimes paid their tuition in produce. Bob Jones Jr. remembered that one student paid his tuition in collards, and the college served them so often that people claimed that BJC stood for "big, juicy collards."[24]

More serious for Jones was his school's bankruptcy in 1933. The corporation that handled the real estate development in connection with the college's founding had transferred mortgages to the school. With the depression the real estate business in Florida declined even further, compounding the bust in the late 1920s. With virtually no income from sales, the school could not meet its bonded indebtedness. Led by a former faculty member who had been fired for liberal theological leanings, some bondholders filed for payment, and Jones, proclaiming "I have done the best I could," filed for bankruptcy with the approval of the board of trustees.[25] Jones had learned a painful lesson. In the future he would avoid debt; financial prudence replaced his zeal for the excesses of the business spirit.

Though not consistently critical of business, fundamentalists in the 1930s occasionally denounced businesspeople and the economic system. Most often the critique made a spiritual point more than an economic one. William Bell Riley found himself agreeing with Father Coughlin, radical Catholic radio priest and enemy of bankers: "The church does not condemn wealth. It does condemn the abuse of wealth." The greed of American bankers, giant economic enterprises "often a robber of thousands and an oppressor of tens of thousands," and "mammon worshiping Americans in pursuit of unearned wealth" all contributed to the depression, Riley argued. Capitalism and human sinfulness had converged; to him both were responsible. Harry A. Ironside, pastor of Moody Church, attacked the "greed and . . . the tyranny of soulless corporations and capitalists preying on the laboring classes." Bob Jones Sr. equated stock market speculation with "a gambling craze" and called the Wall Street crash "a disgrace to the people" due in part to "human weakness." "Instead of trusting God, we trusted the dollar and now we've got it in the neck," Jones declared to an Alabama revival campaign audience. Some say spend, some say save, he continued, some say "stand by the banks, but they don't stand by us." Jones also blamed repeal of prohibition on "great capitalists" who wanted to shift the tax burden to working men.[26]

Others sensed a deeper spiritual problem; the economic crisis represented judgment for sin. Revival was the only solution, not persecution of business. James M. Gray argued in the *Moody Monthly* that although business bore a "fair share" of the blame for the depression, "political demagogues" contributed to the crisis. The selfishness that caused it extended to business, workers, farmers, and professionals. The only remedy, Gray believed, was Christ and ministers proclaiming the Word of God in power. "Perhaps this depression if it continues and grows more serious," he wrote in 1930, "may result in a spiritual revival." Paul W. Rood, editor of the *King's Business,* in citing economist Roger W. Babson's call for a "spiritual awakening" echoed the need for revival as the only remedy. Charles G. Trumbull of the *Sunday School Times* shared a reader's darker scenario: the depression was perhaps preparing the way for the end times, for the Beast or Antichrist, who would bring temporary prosperity, a prelude to Christ's return and kingdom.[27] For many conservative evangelicals of the era, premillennialism never ventured too far from their thoughts.

Some fundamentalists struck at more practical aspects of the economic system, challenging assumptions of the business ethos. Efficiency, an ideal for business and religion in the 1920s, had a downside for some in the depression. Riley observed that the "triumph of modern machinery" led to unemployment: "inventors have upset the whole applecart." Paul Rader railed at technocracy. New technology made industry more productive and turned "millions of people loose with leisure." To him that was not progress, but avoiding work, which God ordained as a curse for sin. Another conservative writer, acknowledging the need for good business, planning, and organization, warned about the "machine spirit," a focus on efficiency in the church. "It is the Holy Spirit who builds the church," he continued. "Here the machine of the technocrat is eliminated." One critic of business noted that in Jesus' parable of the sower, the seed is broadcast, not thrown with "machine-like precision." This tale, a "tragic story of waste and, from the modern point of view, of inefficiency," should instruct the church. Although the tale does not justify waste, it indicates that the church "must ever broadcast the seed of the gospel with a lavish hand."[28]

The consumer society, celebrated by many fundamentalists in the prior decade, had come to symbolize crass materialism for some. Rader denounced standardized American life, which included "forced consumption." The *King's Business* cautioned against the "Peril of Mammonism," calling America's material prosperity "an unmixed blessing. When Christians begin to be controlled by the spirit that says, 'Let us buy, accumulate and enjoy to the full the fruits of our toil in this life,' they are in danger of losing the vision the Master gave them when they were born again." A few months later, after business leaders continued to urge consumer spending, the editor reminded readers that the prodigal son "consumed or dissipated all his substance." "No; we do not need a 'spending spree,'" he continued. In response to calls for new businesses, like automobiles, movies, and radio in the 1920s, to spur consumption, James M. Gray lamented that those items had "congested our streets, corrupted our morals, kept us awake nights, increased our taxes and burdened us with debt." But the average person, Gray continued, "no longer trusts the individuals and the forces . . . that have been manipulating" the American economy.[29]

The businessman ceased being a hero to some. One writer chided the businessman for not coming to church or tithing, for reading his trade paper over his denominational paper. The fictional pastor declared to the businessman: "In short, the question is whether Christianity is your business, [but] I'm afraid it is not." Such a barb would have been rare in the 1920s. Bruce Barton, treated deferentially during the prosperity of the Coolidge years, drew fire on two occasions from Charles G. Trumbull during the 1930s. Barton's books had been "based on the same fundamental unbelief, rejection of the Scriptures, imagination run wild in fiction offered as fact, and a trampling under foot of the Gospel and the blood of Christ." Christ as a "super salesman" appealed to an age of "selling," a time with little interest in faith or repentance, Trumbull reasoned. "No matter that there come times when nobody can sell anything. Never mind the fact that it is the worst metaphor in all the world for Christ and his . . . kingdom . . . where nothing is for sale." A Christian businessman from Iowa even questioned the editor of the *Sunday School Times* about whether Christians should join the Rotary or Kiwanis, since scripture warned about fellowship with unbelievers. Trumbull, dealing with this issue during the depression as he had in the 1920s, reassured him that such associations were appropriate and even necessary for businessmen.[30]

On two separate occasions in the *Moody Monthly* James M. Gray allowed Christian socialists to present their case, followed by his polite rebuttals. Those articles showed how far some fundamentalists had gone in countenancing criticisms of capitalism. It was reminiscent of *The Fundamentals* and its tolerance of socialism. One writer declared that America's economic system was wrong and that the only remedies were the golden rule and for the government to "help the workers and not help the capitalist." In the same magazine another author argued that socialism was closer to the ideal of the first-century Christians than capitalism. Moreover, capitalism was "antichristian" since the Antichrist was interested in business, the buying, selling, and mark of the beast in Revelation 13. Though he allowed the debate, Gray roundly defended private enterprise. As to the Christian socialists, "the emphasis is on the noun rather than the adjective," he presumed. Socialism might work in the millennium, but capitalism worked better in an imperfect world, and he believed that neither system was more Christian than the other. His conclusion to the debate: save souls, stay out of politics, but fight the idea that government should support the people.[31]

Coexisting in the 1930s with doubts about capitalism, a celebration of the business ethos lingered from the 1920s, chastened perhaps by the economic crisis but still indicative of the ambiguity fundamentalists had toward their culture. Paul W. Rood, new editor of the *King's Business,* in 1935 evoked in a stale manner the commercial metaphor for evangelism, reminiscent of the magazine's 1920s rhetoric and Bruce Barton: "Wist ye not that I must be about my Father's business?" H. E. Eavey, in a founder's week address at Moody Bible Institute, echoed the simpler and more spiritual use of the business analogy, harking back to Moody himself. "Go to the Book for merchandising principles," he advised, but "Make Him the great Head of your business." "God cannot trust many people with much money. . . . When we get too much success it doesn't work," he continued. Businesspeople had better trust God, not humans, and most importantly, they should seize all opportunities to witness for Christ. James Gray agreed with one of his readers who argued that the gospel, wherever preached, yielded a "great producing and consuming middle class" whose "moral fiber" was pivotal to industrialism's success. By 1935 Gray recommended that more people in business represent Americans in Congress.[32]

The emphasis on growth survived in the 1930s, and despite the depression, fundamentalist enterprises expanded impressively, as historian Joel A. Carpenter has pointed out, in contrast to mainline denominations, which did not. For three years Wheaton College was the fastest-growing liberal arts college in the nation. James Oliver Buswell presided over the school during this growth, and although he held that the result of a larger Wheaton was "spiritual intensity" and greater educational quality, he talked at some length about the least important reason, from his viewpoint, for growth—"maximum efficiency." The Great Depression had not dimmed his zeal for this feature of corporate America. Buswell asserted that the current enrollment, around one thousand, was the level at which "every dollar begins to bring its maximum results." He recognized the "cold and secular" nature of these points but concluded: "Business efficiency is not an end in itself, but business efficiency in Christian education . . . is indeed a cause for rejoicing." Earlier he had argued for the addition of business courses since the world needed Christian businesspeople and ministers with business skills.[33]

Typical of fundamentalist institutional growth in the 1930s was the Bible school and college movement: twenty-nine new schools were founded in the decade, in contrast to seventeen in the 1920s. Those schools weathered the depression because they had always been operated cheaply, teachers had never been well paid, the leaders were effective fundraisers through churches and radio broadcasts, and the schools were affordable to students. For the fall of 1935 Moody Bible Institute had its largest enrollment in its history to that point. Unlike Moody Bible Institute and others that focused on training church workers and evangelists, William Bell Riley educated men to be pastors. In the 1930s Riley recognized that in supplying ministers, the "market" demanded variety; some churches wanted scholar-preachers, others did not. To meet that market in 1935, he founded a theological seminary, with a greater academic emphasis than his Northwestern Bible School. By the end of the decade he had over a thousand students in the Bible School and seminary.[34]

Fundamentalist businesspeople expanded evangelistic outreaches. In the life of R. G. LeTourneau, the boundaries between evangelicalism and capitalism blurred in such a manner that gave reality to Calvin Coolidge's adage about workers as worshippers and factories as temples. LeTourneau in 1920 had started a heavy machinery manufacturing business that by the late 1930s had expanded to plants in California, Illinois, and Georgia. Gross income in 1936, despite the depression, exceeded four million dollars. For LeTourneau, a layperson, Christ came before business, and his testimony was that all of his company belonged to God. After his conversion he and his pastor had prayed for the Lord's will in his life, and the result was a calling to be "His business man." LeTourneau followed through by officially dedicating his plants to God and usually those services would extend into a week-long revival meeting held inside the plant, accommodating a few thousand people. At one such dedication service at the Peoria, Illinois, plant in 1936, a quartet of employees, all BIOLA graduates, furnished special music. Later, noontime gospel meetings were part of the plant routine. A LeTourneau factory completed in 1939 in Georgia provided jobs for needy Bible students at nearby Toccoa Falls Institute. LeTourneau insisted that his blend of piety and production cloaked no ulterior motives. There was no coercion—he simply sought to reach workingmen for Christ; business success was only a by-product. But he noted with pride that the gospel made contented workers, and "contented employees are poor prospects for a union agitator."[35]

Evangelistic clubs for businessmen continued to flourish. Clarence Macartney in 1930 started a Tuesday Noon Club for Businessmen with twelve men, and attendance grew to two thousand. The interdenominational group met once a week for lunch, a song, and a message. The Christian Men's Evangelistic Club in Charlotte in 1932 sent nine teams of men to minister in the "destitute" sections of the city, hit hard by the depression, to minister to people too embarrassed by their clothes to attend church. Bob Jones Sr.'s evangelistic organization, Gospel Fellowship Association, had on its twenty-member board eleven men involved in business clubs in such states as Washington, Michigan, New York, and throughout the South. The mission was simple: "this greatest business in the world—the winning of lost people." [36]

The recovery and growth of Bob Jones College provided a remarkable success story during the depression. In 1933, following bankruptcy in Florida, the school bought an old Methodist college property in Cleveland, Tennessee, and opened with three hundred students. Cleveland offered a more central location. "If we had goods to sell we wouldn't put them in the basement," Jones told supporters, and "We have something to sell." The Cleveland Chamber of Commerce contributed to the school and was impressed with Jones: "He talked business . . . not as a minister unskilled in the ways of the commercial world." Enrollment outstripped facilities, despite the construction of a new building each year in Cleveland. By 1940 five hundred students, the limit for the school, hailed from forty-four states and eight countries. [37]

The relationship Jones forged with businessman John Sephus Mack contributed to the financial resurgence of the college. The benefactor, president of G. C. Murphy stores, had met Jones in Pennsylvania revival campaigns. In Jones he saw an energetic leader for a "good little school," but ironically he, a businessman, cautioned the evangelist about being too much like a zealous businessman in promoting the college. "When it is all said and done you are a salesman," he wrote to Jones. He chided the evangelist and college president for overselling and being too optimistic, impetuous, and ambitious to build a big school. "But, I do not believe even in the salesmanship," he confided to Jones. Earlier he had reminded him that his "first venture in the college wasn't a success," and he did not want to put money in a losing venture. [38]

In the end Jones proved persuasive as Mack continued to donate to the college. Bob Jones College in Florida did not fail, he argued; the real estate venture connected with it failed. The school relocated in Tennessee for a central geographical location, similar reasoning to how Mack would locate a dime store, he wrote to Mack. "I recognize the fact that I am a salesman and the type work I have always done has schooled me in putting propositions over quickly," he confessed. Even though he was an "enthusiastic propagandist," he was also a Christian and did not seek to put undue pressure on Mack. "I need special warning about overselling what I have. That is my weakness," he acknowledged. Little wonder Jones could tell *Time* magazine in 1937 that some of his college religion majors found it a good education for selling insurance. For Bob Jones, the business ethos seemed to survive the depression intact.[39]

Promotional strategies, popular in the 1920s, succeeded as well in the 1930s. William Bell Riley in 1936 wrote a chapter on advertising for the church. Calling Isaiah, Jeremiah, and Ezekiel more sensational than any modern preacher, including Billy Sunday, Riley cautioned against, not sensation, but "cheap sensation." "Advertising should be sane and snappy," not overdone like P. T. Barnum. Above all it should be honest: "If all the other sins of preachers were pardoned, the one of exaggeration may yet balk some of them at Heaven's gate." Riley had practical suggestions: a series of church meetings was good advertising, like a store or theater that operates daily or frequently; a newspaper was a good promotional source, even critical publicity was valuable; and, finally, church members were the "best mediums of advertising Christianity." In a 1934 revival campaign in Charlotte, North Carolina, Mordecai Ham resorted to sensationalism to promote his meetings. He accused local high school students of frequenting a brothel after one student convert confessed. But Ham got more than he bargained for; angry students, city officials, and a newspaper denounced his attack. Some enemies of Ham even tried to entrap his pianist by planning to send a young boy to his hotel room, but someone at a newspaper overheard the plot and tipped off the pianist. Ham eventually met and reconciled with students, but in the end he accomplished his purpose: he extended the revival campaign for a week.[40]

Bob Jones College advertised aggressively in magazines, typically inside front or back covers, in either full- or half-page ads. The ads cleverly touted the school as a "modern" college in facilities, methods, and standards, using the word "modern" five times in bold type. However, introduced by the word "BUT," the bottom of the ad reminded readers that "There is NO COMPROMISE WITH SO-CALLED MODERNISM." Similar advertising for other fundamentalist schools worked also, as their enrollments grew steadily throughout the decade. Contributions flowed in as well. One reader of the *Sunday School Times* revealed that such consumer society tactics worked: "the advertisements of the Fundamentalist colleges make a heavy pull on my heartstrings, and all I can do about it is to send a couple of dollars occasionally to a Bible Institute."[41]

Fundamentalists continued to "mass market" the gospel successfully with magazines and radio. The *Moody Monthly* had a net increase of 13,000 subscribers during the 1930s and totaled 40,000 by 1940. Other periodicals provided fundamentalist literature and publicity: BIOLA's *King's Business,* Riley's *Pilot,* and Trumbull's *Sunday School Times.* In addition, Jones edited a religious weekly, and J. Frank Norris continued to publish the *Fundamentalist.* Writing in 1939, Carl F. H. Henry, himself a conservative evangelical and sympathetic to fundamentalism, challenged the clergy to make better use of the print media, to have more professional journalistic training for their periodicals, operated mostly by preachers. "Lines of type can become pulpits," he charged; "The church is neglecting the press as an avenue to the masses in this day." Henry's indictment seems a bit extreme today, given the quantity if not quality of fundamentalist ventures in the "word business." [42]

The most successful medium for fundamentalists, however, was radio. There were eighteen million radios in America in 1935, the number having doubled since 1930. By 1938, according to one survey, radio listening had become the nation's number one leisure-time entertainment. Despite the preference of the networks for ecumenical or mainline religious spokespeople, fundamentalists flooded the airwaves, buying time. There were new personalities and programs for the wider audience. An unofficial directory published in 1932 in the *Sunday School Times* listed over 400 evangelical programs on eighty different stations in the nation. By 1939 Moody Bible Institute's WMBI had produced over 35,000 programs in thirteen years of broadcasting. The institute never made "frantic" appeals for funds, but the station received more than 382,700 pieces of mail. In 1939 MBI offered a course in radio broadcasting. The impact was impressive. A visitor from Scotland could startle his MBI audience by declaring that he regularly listened to WMBI programs. Bob Jones Sr. broadcast over twelve stations throughout the country from a radio studio in the college chapel in Cleveland, Tennessee. Wheaton College had a radio program on a local station, and some on campus wanted to be certain that for testimony's sake it was first-class in quality, to showcase the school and Christian scholarship. Martin R. DeHaan's *Radio Bible Class* and Donald Gray Barnhouse's *Bible Study Hour* attracted listeners nationally. [43]

J. Frank Norris proved most unconventional in the use of radio. In the early 1930s he broadcast over a Texas network of eight stations and could be heard as far away as Idaho, where one listener complained that "jazzy, devilish programs" from two West Coast stations interfered with his signal. One of his many critics complained that Norris baptized at midnight those converted over the radio, without church approval. In 1935 Norris, while retaining his Ft. Worth pastorate, became pastor of Detroit's Temple Baptist Church, a move that expanded his base, providing more exposure and revenue. The Detroit church funded his magazine and broadcasts over the 50,000-watt WJR in Detroit.[44]

More respected and successful on the radio was Charles E. Fuller. Starting in the late 1920s as a pastor in a Los Angeles suburb with broadcasts sponsored by his church and BIOLA, Fuller in 1933 entered the radio ministry full-time, and by 1940 his *Old-Fashioned Revival Hour* became the most popular religious radio program in the United States, broadcast over 256 stations with American and foreign listeners totaling fifteen to twenty million. Fuller displayed clever marketing skills. He sent Bibles to children who memorized scripture. Initially shunned by networks, he syndicated his radio program until he joined the Mutual Broadcasting System in 1937. His newsletter communicated with listeners and solicited funds, and he traveled to promote his radio show; in 1938 forty thousand people attended an Easter service at Chicago's Soldier Field. For Charles G. Trumbull, part of Fuller's success came from the fact that he "knows folks" and that he was a "simple-hearted, straight-forward businessman and layman at heart."[45]

Fundamentalists cultivated mass appeal on the air, with speakers copying the rapid-fire style of the radio news reporter or using a more conversational tone, evoking the intimacy of a visitor to the home. Other radio personalities created a family atmosphere, appealed to children, or communicated a folksy earnestness. Shunned by the Columbia Broadcasting System and the National Broadcasting Company, fundamentalists had to work harder for successful programs and audiences. They bought time slots on local stations, and this syndication worked well with their later buying time on new networks, the American Broadcasting Company and the Mutual Broadcasting System.[46]

The fundamentalist affinity for commercial culture between the wars revealed a striking ambiguity toward modernity. Long viewed as simply antimodern, fundamentalists, by adapting to an industrial and consumer society with its premium on secular values such as organization, efficiency, consumption, marketing, and numerical growth, revealed a modern streak of their own. George Marsden described evangelicals as "master . . . of the use of technique—for promotion, advertising, and so forth—in modern culture"; therefore, in some ways they were "very modern people." Martin Marty, though he labeled fundamentalists "counter modernists," acknowledged that evangelism of the early twentieth century was "not afraid of modern techniques." "It was as bureaucratized and rationalized as anything Max Weber was portraying in business and government," he added. In the 1920s, Marty concluded that fundamentalists "made at least one great exception in their negation of the world: nationalism, and with it support of America's economic system." James Davison Hunter has argued that between modernity and religion a "mutual accommodation" takes place, and critically it was in business, a key part of modernization, where fundamentalists adapted most; the resources they developed—institutions and technologies—allowed them to more than hold their own against traditional elites.[47]

One critic, Robert A. Wauzzinski, has charged that fundamentalism-evangelicalism even aided the process of secularization by uncritically accepting capitalism and rejecting socialism. Evangelicalism and capitalism focused on individualism, he argued, to the detriment of the organic view of man, which is more consistent with scripture as well as classical Christian theorists and reformers. The result, according to Wauzzinski, is a faith captive to culture.[48]

On the other hand, it was not merely a one-way street toward secularization. Leigh Schmidt, in his study of consumerism, religion, and holidays, concluded that the relationship between Christianity and the consumer culture was so complex, "by turns, symbiotic and conflictual, complementary and contested," that Christians both participated in and criticized this culture. Also, not only were they altered by it, but so was the marketplace. "In this story," he observed, "the sacred and secular have often reversed themselves, the marketplace becoming a realm of religious enchantment and the churches a site of material abundance and promotional gimmicks." Schmidt was struck by "how secular much of the sacred is and how sacred much of the secular is." Fundamentalists, by their participation, may have tempered the world of business.[49]

Far worse, for some critics, than the failure to challenge capitalism's secular values was the fundamentalist-evangelical imitation of business. Despite the clear conflict between biblical teachings and the business spirit of the churches in the 1920s, Rolf Lundén observed that churches generally did not threaten materialism. Confronting the business ethos perhaps would have been "impractical and would cost too much," he conjectured. Religion became for too many a commodity to be consumed in order that the "customer" would be happier; the consumer society, therapeutic culture, and religion coexisted too easily. There were occasional exceptions. One minister warned in the 1920s, with a sermon titled "The Dangerous Glamor of Prosperity," against the "obtuseness of Christians in their failure to see the inconsistency and danger in thus conforming to the modern mode of life," with some Christians having three houses and the latest models of the most expensive automobiles. Bob Jones Sr. despaired that despite our luxuries "we are no happier than our grandparents were," because our spiritual growth had not kept pace with our material growth.[50]

In a revival sermon Paul Rader announced that old-time evangelists "ranted and raved against dancing," but he was no longer going to do that. "The day of negatives is past," he concluded. For Rader and other fundamentalists, did the lure of the marketplace soften the message? Unquestionably, for some it did. To attract numbers of people in print and on radio, as well as in person, to reach and satisfy middle-class America trained in the ways of consumption, messages for some preachers became simpler, broader, generally evangelical, nonsectarian, less abrasive and less pietistic, as religious activities overwhelmed devotional life.[51]

In succumbing to the business culture, fundamentalists followed the general pattern of all Protestant churches in the 1920s; as Rolf Lundén discovered, the American economic order generally was uncritically accepted by churches. Susan Curtis has determined that social gospelers by the 1920s had merged comfortably with the consumer society. Even the liberal Protestant giant Harry Emerson Fosdick partially accommodated to the spirit of Barton. Given modernist notions about the immanence of Christ in the culture, their adjustments seem less startling than for the fundamentalists who argued that their faith transcended their culture.

There were dissenters: on the left Reinhold and Richard Niebuhr criticized capitalism, and on the right holiness groups did not mimic the material ways of the middle class.[52]

In the end, fundamentalists generally reflected the attitude of secular culture toward business, adoring during the 1920s and slightly tempered in the 1930s by the Great Depression. During the 1930s, while their general embrace of business continued, they were occasionally critical of greed, unemployment due to technological advances, and the materialism of the consumer society. Some fundamentalist ministries nursed their own financial woes. Many saw the nation's economic troubles in broader spiritual terms as God's judgment. For them, as a whole, as far as business was concerned, there was no "great reversal"; their love of business continued from the late nineteenth century through the 1930s and beyond. Affection for free enterprise placed them in the mainstream of American culture, which was not true for other views of theirs, such as rejection of modern science. Infatuation with the business ethos had continued from the Progressive Era, which valued efficiency and organization. Worship of the businessman also reinforced the turn-of-the-century "muscular Christianity" movement.

Perhaps there were earlier precedents. Fundamentalists merely continued the promotion necessary to build a voluntary, "gathered" church, essential since colonial days with the demise of the parish system. Like nineteenth-century Methodists after the end of the established church, they took advantage of a revolution in the religious marketplace, creating new organizations to rival mainline denominations. Richard Carwardine noted that those Methodists suffered no problems with their "embourgeoisement," despite their lower-class origins, because they had embraced "enterprise and the capitalist ethic." Such a linkage spared fundamentalists the antimodern fate of Primitive Baptists, Mennonites, or Amish.[53]

Fundamentalists and evangelicals sought to Christianize business and businesspeople, a part of society viewed by them and others as perhaps inherently superior and therefore a worthy target. Moreover, the affinity between evangelism and selling was too strong. "Fundamentalists were principled market men who asked for no subsidies from the government or from media," historian R. Laurence Moore reasoned. "They sold religion the old-fashioned way, except that they took full advantage of technology," he continued. As they sought to save souls, fundamentalists could be pragmatic. Moore concluded that "religion, with the various ways it has entered the cultural marketplace, has been more inventive than its detractors imagined. As an independent influence, it won some important victories. And as a commodity, it satisfied many buyers." [54]

Despite good intentions, fundamentalists paid a price. Their wholeness or integrity had been diminished. Contradictions abounded. A spiritual movement had embraced secular strategies. They looked and behaved increasingly like the modern world they decried. All varieties of fundamentalists fell prey, from the pietistic ones to the revivalists. As they anticipated the millennial return of Christ, they too often had ignored the admonition of the Apostle Paul, "be not conformed to this world" (Romans 12:2).

3 Encountering Popular Culture

The relationship between a believer and the world the believer inhabits has been a central dilemma for Christians through the ages, from Christian asceticism of the ancient world to Protestant disdain of amusements in the modern age. In addition to theological differences with the modernists, fundamentalists sought also to distinguish themselves as much as possible from modern, secular culture, thereby maintaining that tension. With rapid urbanization providing unprecedented temptations, they emphasized personal holiness as they tried to reject the "worldliness" around them. Charles G. Trumbull, at the brink of the postwar era, reminded readers of the Apostle John's admonition "Love not the world" but carefully added: "It is of course impossible to lay down a hard and fast line, to say this is worldly, and that is not. But, speaking generally, worldliness betrays itself in its atmosphere. There is a something undefined, perhaps indefinable, and yet very real." In the 1920s and 1930s conservative evangelicals, similarly ambivalent toward their secular environs, not surprisingly condemned it but amazingly also at times imitated it.[1]

Christians had struggled against the world's amusements for ages. The medieval church and the reformer John Calvin condemned dancing. Late-sixteenth-century English Protestant reformer John Northbrooke attacked, along with dance, stage plays, cards, dice, and cockfights. Colonial Puritan divine Increase Mather continued the tradition. Anglican revivalist George Whitefield exhorted listeners to turn from worldliness in the eighteenth century. In the Second Great Awakening in the nineteenth century, Charles Finney emphasized personal holiness and opposed worldly amusements, particularly those in the city; he argued that virtually all amusements were suspect. According to historian Ann Wagner, from 1840 to 1860 mainstream American Protestant clergy of all denominations launched unprecedented attacks on amusements—dance, theater, cards, novels, horse racing, and the circus. By the late nineteenth century and early twentieth century new social conditions—growing urbanization, immigration, more commercial amusements, movies, and working women—brought greater temptations and opposition. By the 1920s fundamentalists encountered a popular culture thoroughly embedded in American life, and personal holiness, marked by prayer, Bible reading, church attendance, and separation from the world, became increasingly difficult.[2]

Between the wars, fundamentalists sought to uphold nineteenth-century evangelical behavioral standards. In doing so, they reflected the influence of the late-nineteenth-century Wesleyan holiness movement, with its revivalism and emphasis on personal piety, although fundamentalist conduct codes generally were not as strict as the holiness groups. But like their holiness brethren, they sought separation from a world increasingly hostile to their views and built institutions—churches, schools, and church-related organizations—to serve as havens. They tightened the moral guidelines that had been more fluid for previous generations. Alcohol, profanity, dancing, popular music, theater, tobacco, cards, gambling, work on Sunday, and, for some, even play on Sunday remained taboo. Movies were forbidden. Ministers emphasized modest dress and light makeup for females. In response to greater permissiveness in the culture, fundamentalists stressed sexual purity. Their goal was a wholesome "look" and life. By the 1930s their Bible schools and colleges had codified many of these standards into strict behavioral codes.[3]

Cultural historians disagree about definitions of *mass culture, popular culture,* and *consumer culture.* Michael Kammen has argued that even with significant overlapping, popular and mass culture can be distinguished by scale, chronology, and the nature of the activity. Popular culture is more limited in scale, reached its height between 1885 and 1935 (mass culture developed after World War II with television), and is more participatory (mass culture is more passive). In the 1920s, Kammen also has argued, consumer culture thrived, with public relations and advertising gaining prominence. With advertising in magazines and on radio, the line between commercial culture and popular culture blurred. The resulting combination of consumer culture and popular culture, for the purposes of this study, will be called mass culture. Furthermore, mass culture can be distinguished from the highbrow view of culture as refinement and the even more inclusive definition of culture as the sum total of a people's beliefs and values, a perspective favored by anthropologists. The fundamentalist terminology for popular culture was "the world," "worldliness," or citing the specific attraction, for example, the movies. In the interwar years a fundamentalist tradition of personal holiness and piety encountered popular amusements, ranging from jazz, theater, and movies to radio. Fundamentalists also coped with one consequence of that social whirl, the flapper, the new woman.[4]

After World War I, fundamentalists viewed with alarm the lure of entertainment and leisure; it was a time of spiritual and cultural crisis. Victorian traditions faced numerous threats from modern culture; the civil battled the savage. Popular arts had exploded, with many magazines having circulations in the millions; radio sets, which totaled several million in the mid-1920s, jumped to twenty-five million by World War II; and movies with sound attracted seventy to eighty million viewers weekly. Christians yearned for absolutes in morals, elevated home and family, honored separate gender roles, and favored the classics in art and literature. They strove to maintain nineteenth-century evangelical moral standards. To them the secular world increasingly tilted toward relativity in ethics, lawlessness in the arts and culture, and altered the roles of men and women. The home, so vital to Victorian America, was vulnerable. Likewise, the Victorian "cult of character"—a range of virtues described by one scholar as "dependably self-controlled, punctual, orderly, hard working, conscientious, sober . . . ready to postpone immediate gratification for long-term goals, pious . . . a believer in the truth of the Bible, oriented strongly toward home and family, honorable . . . anxious for self-improvement . . . and patriotic"—seemed endangered. Some fundamentalists even denied that the modern age could secularize their world. Social historian Ted Ownby has argued that Protestants in theory "did not divide the world into sacred and nonsacred spheres." "Life is not divided into the secular and the sacred," Bob Jones Sr. often declared to his chapel audience. "For a Christian, everything in life is sacred. All ground is holy ground, every bush a burning bush, and every place a Christian is, the temple of God is there." A Wheaton College partisan cautioned that "Too rigid a distinction between the sacred and secular cannot be drawn; however, in the Wheaton atmosphere the sacred . . . did not become secular, but the 'secular' did become sacred." [5]

The postwar era loomed as a critical era. "We are now witnessing the widest wave of immorality in the history of the human race," declared John Roach Straton with some exaggeration. Young people were a particular concern for fundamentalists. In his 1926 inaugural address at Wheaton College, President James O. Buswell focused attention on moral laxness and observed that the young usually do not lose their faith through intellectual problems but through sensual pleasures and amusements. The modern world, he continued, is "deluged" with impurities— the theater, dancing, card playing—through which young people become "spiritually anemic." Ten years ago evangelical churches and colleges had denounced those activities, but after the war, with conditions ten times worse, they tolerated the activities, he believed. Bob Jones Sr. surveyed the sensuality, lawlessness, and juvenile delinquency of the interwar years and concluded that "Now all hell has broken loose." Will H. Houghton explained the prison suicide of an eighteen-year-old boy who had confessed to thirty-five robberies: "A cigarette-soaked brain, no doubt, and a mind saturated with moving picture conceptions of love, form the background of this sordid story." [6]

The allure of popular culture threatened not only youth but also the home, "the backbone of civilization," as one minister termed it. Clarence E. Macartney worried especially about the decline of the Christian home, calling it the most important school, church, or club. Though a bachelor, he believed that if the gospel were to change culture, the home and the church had to do it together. Louis T. Talbot, pastor of the Los Angeles Church of the Open Door, argued, "It is very difficult for a boy or girl to go to hell, if he has lived in a home for eighteen years where the Bible has been consistently honored in daily life as well as read at the family altar." Many, like Reverend T. C. Horton, lamented the passing of the "old-fashioned home" with a Bible on the center table: "There was no rattle of the auto with its tooting horn; no radio jazz; no call from the movies; but there was . . . a sense of harmony and one-ness." An array of evils—dance, jazz, novels, magazines, liquor, divorce, movies, radio, the automobile—lurked in mass culture, and all seemed to threaten the home. Reverend Harold L. Lundquist of Chicago bemoaned the "superfluous" modern home and complained that people are "courted in an automobile, married in a church, spend our days in an office or on the golf course, attend some place of amusement at night . . . and are buried from a funeral home." "What is the end of it going to be for a godless, pleasure-loving, carousing, gambling, home-wrecking generation?" wondered the *Moody Monthly* editorially. For some fundamentalists, popular culture seemed to overwhelm them.[7]

Furthermore, in cities the temptations from entertainment and leisure abounded. The image of the evil city, persistent in Western civilization from ancient to modern days, gained strength in the late nineteenth century among conservative evangelicals as industrialization and immigration greatly urbanized America. Racial and religious prejudice toward Catholic and Jewish immigrants, common in American culture in the era, intensified the fundamentalists' anti-urban bias. The cities fashioned a new culture, one that challenged Victorianism. "Urban life disrupted the sense of religious continuity and tradition present in other times and places," historian Nancy T. Ammerman has concluded. "It was in the cities that the challenge to Protestant ideas and hegemony was most clear." By 1920 America had become more urban than rural, and fundamentalists recognized danger. John Roach Straton ministered in what he labeled "Babylon," a "pagan city." "We must either Americanize and Christianize New York, or New York will speedily Europeanize and paganize us!" with its threats to the Sabbath, the home, and "our Anglo-Saxon life," he warned. Sunday, he pointed out, was the most popular "recreation day" of the week: one Sunday evening in the Times Square district 1,817 people attended church, but 75,000 enjoyed the theaters and movies. Even worse, he added, the problem with New York City is the problem for the entire United States: "we are on a joy ride when we ought to be at a prayer meeting! Our people are money mad and pleasure crazed." J. Gresham Machen, reflecting on the same city from the 102nd floor of the Empire State Building, saw an age that was a slave to greed and passion, forgetting

God, with "its towering architecture a symbol of its spiritual bankruptcy," a "rebellious tower of Babel seeking to reach unto heaven by human pride." He found New York to be a "strange city," "magnificently ugly," and added, "It seemed like some weird, tortured imagination of things in another world."[8]

Charles Blanchard, visiting Chicago, noted "poor faces so poisoned with tobacco and liquor," "more miseries in the world than ever before," and "more creature comfort," too. With the love of pleasure demonstrated by young people, he despaired of the future. Paul Rader, Chicago-based evangelist-pastor, decried the affluence, luxury, lust, and crime that seemed to coexist in 1920s America: "A city is insane when it disregards its moral cleanness." William Bell Riley, who pastored a downtown church in Minneapolis, called the inner city "darkest America," where the "sin-stricken and suffering crowded together." Cities proved, he believed, that corruption multiplied. "Today, Satan's throne is at the city's center," and a "brood of iniquities flourish" around the four hundred saloons in Minneapolis, he added.[9]

Many fundamentalists revealed an anti-urban bias as they waxed nostalgic about rural life, for some a place untainted by the world. Ted Ownby has observed that for rural southern evangelicals, towns were places of sin and economic necessity; the railroad and consumerism brought the urban and rural worlds into closer contact. The resulting reform efforts of prohibition and protecting the Sabbath were rural evangelical efforts to curb "sins" in the towns and cities. Bob Jones Sr., a product of rural southeast Alabama, fretted that Americans had forsaken the "old time country idea of God and decency" and that cities of America had the "same element of degeneracy and decay" as ancient Greece and Rome. "When I was a boy in the country," he continued, "you could have one thing in the city and something else in the country. But how times have changed! Paved highways, automobiles, and modern travel have eliminated the distance between the city and the country." With influences like the "picture shows," cities permeated the rural areas, destroying the Sabbath, "one of the strongest pillars in our civilization."[10]

Straton, also with southern roots, remembered driving his automobile in the country and seeing through a farmhouse window a family at the fireside having evening prayers, and he contrasted that with the "godlessness, self-will and sensuality which we see on every side in the city." Riley, son of a Kentucky farmer and until age twenty-five a farmer himself, declared that "the farm presents the cleanest moral atmosphere" and "contributes to the most even happiness known to the human race." "Man," he added, "has never discovered a better location." Several years later he noted that while country churches were closing because of fewer farmer preachers, the urban "cultured" class, lured away by Sunday golf and motoring, did not attend church as much.[11]

Paradoxically, the most prominent fundamentalist ministries were urban, where, repelled by the secular culture, they were compelled to preach the gospel, both to save souls and rescue city dwellers from the grip of popular evils. Paul W. Rood, ministering in Los Angeles, pointed out that Christ wept over Jerusalem and that Paul preached in Corinth, Ephesus, and Rome; likewise, for today the "problem of evangelizing America is, to a large extent a city problem, for as fare the cities, so fares the nation." In nearby San Diego John Bunyan Smith, pastor of First Baptist Church, organized the Exposition Evangelistic Campaign, 167 consecutive nights of meetings, to coincide with the 1935 California Pacific International Exposition. His church, only six blocks from the fair grounds, sought to reach tourists and navy men as they flocked to San Diego's fair, striving to use a major attraction of popular culture to evangelize, similar to Moody's efforts in Chicago during its 1893 World's Fair. "The evangelization of the city is one of the boldest challenges Christ has ever given to His church," Pastor Smith believed. "Shall our cities be pagan, or shall they be evangelized?" The urban ministry could be personal as well. Young people from Straton's Calvary Baptist Church in New York City were street preaching on 8th Avenue when a young woman, after hearing a familiar childhood hymn, came from a corner saloon and was converted.[12]

Bob Jones Sr. had a twofold strategy for urban redemption. One was the traditional evangelistic campaign. For example, after a 1922 effort in St. Petersburg, Florida, one reporter concluded that a Bob Jones campaign had raised the "general moral tone of the community." Citizens of that city did not want the "fast crowd" of other Florida resorts connected with sports and gamblers. Furthermore, there were no Sunday motion picture theaters or baseball games in St. Petersburg. Jones also foresaw a long-term solution perhaps to urban corruption—building a college as a utopian city. "There was in the evangelist's mind," according to the promotional brochure for the initial construction of his college in Florida, "the vision of a city and college built to the specifications of dreams. . . . the dreamer-evangelist saw the spires of a great Christian college . . . 'Round about it, his eyes could see a model city—a city of homes, and schools and churches—a city permeated with the spirit of a religious renaissance—a city at whose gateway was flung down the gauntlet to modernism." For this Methodist evangelist, perfectionism and agrarianism had made peace with urbanization in modern America.[13]

If Jones viewed his college as an answer to the urban crisis, many fundamentalists viewed their colleges and Bible schools as bulwarks against the corruption of mass culture. Evidence of a crisis and the need for holiness was clear to Charles Blanchard, Wheaton College president. He recalled the late-nineteenth-century colleges that did not tolerate dances, theater, tobacco, or alcohol, but by the early twentieth century, with dances, dramatic clubs, and smokers, they were a "far cry from the college life of those days." In 1919 he surveyed about fifty Midwestern colleges, and an equal number of respondents, thirty-two, denounced card playing and affirmed the inspiration of scripture. Although twenty-eight rejected dancing, only ten responded negatively to evolution. Cultural issues ranked as high or higher than theological or philosophical concerns.[14]

Under its new president, James O. Buswell, installed in 1926, Wheaton continued as a bulwark against worldliness. Although he did not condemn those who disagreed and did not appear self-righteous or superior, Buswell reaffirmed a conservative standard of conduct because he believed that human nature was sinful and that the stage had not been purified. Dance remained unwholesome, gambling was still wrong, and cigarettes were still considered narcotic. "We sacrifice nothing" at Wheaton by giving up amusements, he declared, adding, "At His right hand there are pleasures forevermore." Some Wheaton alumni criticized Buswell for be

ing stricter than Blanchard, but he responded that the standards were necessary because enrollments had increased dramatically, and the outside world had become more immoral. Administration officials defended rules not only on a moral basis but also to make campus life more efficient. Social life involved chaperones, curfews, and bans on automobiles and plays, and opera was suspect. Helen Torrey Renich, student in the 1930s, remembered life there as "a little tight." Students did play Rook all hours of the night with little difficulty, but any students caught not complying with the conduct code would be expelled.[15]

In founding his college in 1927, Bob Jones Sr. promised that its discipline would be "that of a well-ordered home." The school's cultural entertainment would be the "highest type" so students would not care for popular amusements. One faculty member acknowledged that the "godliness of each member of the faculty is placed above scholarship," although scholarship is "not overlooked by any means." Rules prohibited hazing, gambling, drinking, profanity, or use of tobacco on campus. Automobiles were used only for business, and girls had to have chaperones for "social occasions." Students had to check in and out when leaving campus and pledged to report violations to a student-faculty committee. A disgruntled former faculty member depicted Bob Jones College as a "sterilized spot in an infected world," recalling that it "reeks with spiritual disinfection." For her the school had an "almost hysterical awareness of sin." "They graduate boys and girls knowing more of philandering than philosophy, and more of evil than evolution," she lamented.[16]

As the crisis with secular culture intensified after World War I, fundamentalists increasingly rejected obvious threats to the notions of morality. Some of this revulsion was driven by a strong holiness tradition, prominent among evangelicals from late in the previous century. Putting emphasis on the Holy Spirit, sanctification, piety, and separation from the "world" led fundamentalists to think more carefully about the potential "contamination" around them. J. C. Massee defined holiness as "the fountain from which the stream of right conduct flows" and the "death of worldliness." After World War I, historian Robert Moats Miller has observed, "Much of the moral indignation of the [mainline] churches was expended on personal sins to the neglect of any searching analysis of the social order." Fundamentalists were an exaggeration of that trend.[17]

The *Methodist* claimed that for most people in 1930, twenty-two cents out of the dollar went for luxuries and one cent for religion. With the belief that churches had to entertain to attract an audience, many pastors tapped various forms of high and low culture for their services. This trend drew the ire of many fundamentalists. "The church of God has gone into the entertainment business! People must be amused . . . [because] the church needs the money. So the picture-show and the entertainment, in the form of musicales (sacred, perhaps!) and minstrel-show, take the place of the gospel address and the solemn worship of God," lamented H. A. Ironside. To R. A. Torrey it was "startling" that a church thought the gospel had so "lost its power to draw" that it needed amusements to attract a crowd. Reverend R. Banes Anderson also decried entertainment as an attempt to reverse dwindling attendance. The church was not the place for it; moreover, the church could not compete with the world with its secular techniques. People do not attend church because they are not born again, and no amusement could change that, he declared.[18]

Fundamentalists feared that secular amusements threatened the sanctity of the Sabbath. "What a harvest is awaiting the votaries of twentieth century civilization in the day when they must give account!" warned James M. Gray, critical of the motion picture, automobile, radio, and Sunday newspaper for keeping people, even Christians, away from church. For some, the Sunday newspaper was a menace since it kept newsboys from Sunday school and church, diverted readers from attending as well, and provided unnecessary worldly thoughts on Sunday. The Sabbath was for rest and worship, not work or amusement.[19]

The biggest moral issue for the era, of course, was liquor, and there was little middle ground. Buswell held a rather honest, thoughtful, but rigid view of the question, typical of fundamentalists. Although conceding that the Bible may not teach total abstinence and that "moderate" use may be acceptable in certain cultures, in America, where there was no tradition of moderate use of alcohol, abstinence should rule. Then, tapping a kind of cultural relativism of his modernist contemporaries, Buswell argued that even if Christ drank alcoholic wine, that does not mean Americans should today. Alcohol was a different problem for the modern world than the ancient, he continued. "Conditions have changed," moderns are "fast-living people," and the "nervous systems are affected," Buswell concluded. Most of the other conservative religious opponents of strong drink did not bother with such strained arguments; alcohol was wrong, pure and simple. Some separatist Presbyterians, mainly those associated with Machen and Westminster Seminary, argued that since drinking was not specifically prohibited in scripture, the principle of Christian liberty left the choice to the individual.[20]

Cigarettes also were a categorical evil, a threat to health and morals. According to J. C. Massee, cigarettes give the smoker's face a "yellow cast" and "debase his judgment, inflame his passions, and pervert his imaginations." Professor F. E. West of the Bob Jones College science department was persuaded that nicotine was poison and raised blood pressure; moreover, smoking "weakens the heart and causes it to miss a beat now and then," blackens the lungs, and contributes to infant mortality. Critics pointed to advertising by celebrities to attract women and children to cigarettes. Other ministers denounced it as a poor testimony.[21]

Gambling was universally condemned. "Card playing," A. C. Dixon declared, "is a mouse nest in Christian life." It wastes time, and since it depends, not on skill and work, but on chance, it tends to make people dishonest. Card playing, he continued, could lead to gambling and "evil associations." Others made similar attacks: gambling was stealing, it was avaricious, and it could culminate in broken homes, alcoholism, and sexual immorality.[22]

Fundamentalists also targeted the modern dance as unmitigated evil. The issue was not the religious dance of the Bible, the square dance, or dance as exercise or genteel culture, but the immoral modern dance where, according to A. C. Dixon, "the central source of the attraction . . . is sex." For Straton, "The greatest danger point today is in the relationship between the sexes, under the conditions of our congested, overwrought modern life," and the associations with dancing were all bad—embracing, sensuous music, jazz, cigarette smoking, liquor, short dresses, prostitutes, and pimps. "Oh, what tragedies may be laid at the door of the modern dance!" exclaimed James M. Gray. Bob Jones Sr. declared the dance hall as bad as the saloon. In a 1922 St. Petersburg, Florida, campaign he ordered all men and women out of the choir and to "sit with the sinners" if they would not promise to quit dancing. Furthermore, Jones advised, if a man was not affected by dancing, he should send for the family physician. But Bob Shuler summed up the moral issue most succinctly with the question, "can a dancing foot and a praying knee go together?" Fundamentalists were not alone in the critique. Studies of dance halls in the 1920s by social scientists found they were associated with "degraded mores in volume" ranging from marital problems, unwed mothers, and illness to unemployment and poverty. Dancing had become more than a symbol of rejecting traditional moral standards.[23]

■

For all the fundamentalist fury toward secular culture, condemnation of it was only part of the story. A closer look reveals an ambiguity toward popular culture; efforts to control or censor it coexisted along with desires to participate in, accommodate to, and even compete with many features of the "world" that they denounced. This tension not only altered in some cases their cultural context, but it forever changed them as well. Martin Marty noted that as fundamentalists focused on issues related to personal morals, they "picked and chose their way through the culture." In the end, they selectively rejected aspects of leisure and entertainment.[24]

In fact, the equivocation originated in their heritage. Church itself, especially revival meetings, provided spiritual nourishment but also social entertainment approved by the church, and the typically acceptable secular recreations were those endorsed by the church and family—picnics, visiting, and courting. Chautauqua, founded by Methodists to train Sunday school teachers and rooted in camp meetings, became a place of entertainment, a prominent cultural institution in the United States around the end of the nineteenth century. Recognizing an inherent conflict, Charles G. Trumbull, a foremost holiness advocate, advised believers not to fear "healthy amusements of the right sort," not to be priggish, and to beware of the "peril of narrowness in the Victorious Life." He called for a balance between the spiritual and the real world: "Let us deliberately make it our business to cultivate certain secular, human interests." For Trumbull, those could be hobbies, nature, study, and music other than hymns.[25]

But one writer pointed out that the New Testament gave "no categorical answer to these social questions"; there were no "vest pocket rules." Each person, he continued, must use prayer to decide his own principles; otherwise, "your religion spoils your pleasure and your pleasure your religion." A. C. Dixon's principles reflected the arbitrariness of some fundamentalists. Good amusements were those outdoors or without evil associations: golf, tennis, bicycle riding, rowing, hiking, chess, checkers, ping pong, some card games, conversation, some music, and reading masterpieces. Billiards, "kissing games," opera, and the theater all had evil associations and should be avoided. Arno Gaebelein's household did not follow the same guidelines. A cultured man who had a library of two thousand books and who played classical piano music early Sunday mornings, Gaebelein, of German background, enjoyed an occasional beer with his meals and allowed his son Frank to attend the movies and theater. Moody Bible Institute tapped into this confusion about the "new leisure" most imaginatively perhaps by urging its magazine readers to enroll in its Correspondence School, to use their "leisure creatively," and thereby to equip themselves for greater service to Christ.[26]

Several aspects of popular culture mirrored this confusion within the minds of fundamentalists. As illustrated by Billy Sunday, there had been a vital affinity between religion and mass spectator sports for many, whereas others were skeptical or antagonistic. "The most popular man is, not the preacher, but the wrestler, the prize fighter or the baseball player," thundered evangelist Mordecai Ham. Straton denounced boxing as animal-like. For him the body was the temple of the Holy Ghost, and boxing desecrated it with brutality. Its appeal reflected the "insane stampede of this age for pleasure." The saddest aspect of one prizefight, for Straton, was the attendance of even church women, who were watching almost naked men.[27]

But Straton did attend the Dempsey-Carpentier fight in 1921 in order to rebuke it, putting himself "on the firing line for God." Later Straton attacked the fight in what the *New York Times* described as an entertaining sermon. The newspaper challenged: "Why should the good man be so hard on a performance that inspired his own?" Christian colleges had mixed feelings, too, about sports. Wheaton College occasionally had banned football, with President Blanchard denouncing its brutality, but the college reinstated it in 1914. The purpose of Wheaton is not to "furnish amusement for thousands," its alumni magazine editor declared, but "wholesome sport is beneficial," and with clean play and prayer before the game, who could object? George Mueller, renowned for his piety, actually endorsed Sunday athletics, even addressed Sunday baseball games. Sunday, he believed, was a day to get outdoors. No young man, he continued, is going to spend Sunday afternoon in his room reading the Bible. If he did, Mueller figured, there was something abnormal about him.[28]

Summer Bible conferences provided an opportunity, especially for rank-and-file fundamentalists, to blend religion and recreation during a summer vacation. The automobile had made resorts accessible to average Americans, and many Christians flocked to sites in the mountains of Colorado and North Carolina, to the hills of Pennsylvania, to the New Jersey shore, to New England, to the Pacific Northwest, or to Southern California, to enjoy Bible teaching from leading fundamentalists in a setting that combined a modern resort with a camp-meeting atmosphere. Session topics not only covered religion and sacred music but also targeted young people and businesspeople. Despite the Great Depression, the Bible conference movement grew dramatically. In 1930, twenty-seven sites included eighty-eight sessions, but by 1941 the numbers had grown to more than fifty sites and over two hundred sessions.[29]

One of the most popular summer Bible conferences was the Winona Lake Bible Conference in Indiana. There the boundary between faith and leisure blurred as thousands rented cottages at this religious resort. From seven in the morning until ten in the evening the conference typically offered about a dozen sessions, and participants may have listened to as many as six sermons or Bible lessons during one day. Winona Lake was home for Billy Sunday and his song leader, Homer Rodeheaver. Bible conferences like Winona Lake not only refreshed believers spiritually and physically but also strengthened the interdenominational character of fundamentalists as Baptists, Methodists, Presbyterians, and members of other Protestant denominations mingled. Young people also participated actively in the conference movement, with many of them being converted there and later going on to fundamentalist colleges, the pastorate, or the mission field.[30]

Another early form of tension that leisure produced for evangelicals arose from the world of print media—newspapers, magazines, and novels. For one critic the Sunday newspaper had become a "powerful factor in the secularization of Sunday." In homes the father read the news and stocks, the mother the sales and fashions, and the children the comics. "A family which has saturated itself with the Sunday newspaper is in no mood for churchgoing," he added. This amusement threatened the Sabbath for many believers. Likewise, magazines, many of them religious in origin but later shifting far from their earlier Christian views, represented a channel for unbiblical values. Not only did secular periodicals offer what Straton termed "loathsome" and "moral sewage," sensual in words and pictures, but, according to the *Sunday School Times,* popular American magazines increasingly had become antagonistic toward "fundamental Christianity." Citing the Hoover Committee's *Recent Social Trends in the United States,* the *Sunday School Times* reported that "in periodicals listed in the *Reader's Guide,* the percentage of articles indicating an 'approving attitude' toward 'traditional' or fundamental Christianity declined from 78 in 1905 to 33 in 1930." [31]

One fundamentalist identified the "novel reading spirit" as "pernicious." It could "intoxicate the imagination," particularly French novels that were realistic about "uncleanness." The *Sunday School Times* also struck at the realism in modern literature. The short story reader of the 1920s would not recognize the world of "purity, honor, and duty" in the literature of the 1870s and 1880s. "His present habitat is a humid, hectic plain where unnatural mothers, selfish, impudent children, and disloyal husbands and wives poison the air with their moral malaria," its editor opined. "We cannot look for a . . . cleansing of the common reading matter of the people until the Holy Spirit, the Author of the fine arts as well as of ethics, holds deeper sway in the hearts of men," he concluded. [32] Secular, nonfundamentalist critics of realism and naturalism in literature decried its lack of idealism and in that sense found common cause with religious conservatives.

Although they decried the world of secular publishing, fundamentalists understood its power. A century earlier evangelist Charles G. Finney had attacked novel reading yet embraced its format for revivalist theology, for which he was criticized by elites. Evangelicals and fundamentalists, according to William D. Romanowski, had a similar approach: "condemn the content of the popular arts but justify their employment of entertainment media and formats by an appeal to a higher 'sacred' purpose." Looking back in 1940, fifty years since his first volume came out, William Bell Riley believed the printed page was more potent than radio; Bible sales testified to that point. Some of his books, he thought, had reached one hundred thousand people with a specific message. Knowing the power of motion pictures on the public, Paul Rader wrote novels that he hoped were equally dramatic in depicting the Bible. Many Bible schools ran publishing houses and distribution centers, most notably Moody's Bible Institute Colportage Association. Publishers furnished Sunday school materials for those displeased with lessons of the old-line denominations. Also, magazines promoted the schools and provided reading matter for laypeople: the *Moody Monthly, King's Business* of BIOLA, *Pilot* of Riley's Northwestern Schools, along with many others. In 1931, a giant in religious publishing, Fleming H. Revell, died after more than sixty years of producing books that, according to one admirer, "must be worth while, clean, readable, meeting a real demand." This Presbyterian elder, brother-in-law to Moody, had established his headquarters at a Fifth Avenue address in New York City. Religious conservatives could compete with the best the secular world offered in print. Smaller and more typical were publishers like Loizeau Brothers, William Eerdmans Publishing Company, and Zondervan Publishing House.[33]

Fundamentalist reaction to the theater was a bit more complicated. In the ongoing battle between their adapting the forms of secular culture but rejecting its substance as evil, print media posed no problem since the content could be Christianized. With the theater, however, some condemned it wholesale, some sanitized it for religious purposes, and others praised secular drama as worthwhile. According to one scholar, George Whitefield, a British evangelist in America in the eighteenth century, utilized elements of theater and drama that help explain his huge appeal in his day. Before radio and movies became mass media in the 1920s and 1930s, Billy Sunday, with his fiery, colorful histrionics, entertained in a way that for some rivaled vaudeville. Therefore, for conservative Christians, consciously or not, thespian concerns were never far away.[34]

Those fundamentalists who fought the theater had church history on their side. Second-century church father Tertullian condemned it for being too much like pagan Rome. Calvin banned it from Geneva. Puritans opposed it in Elizabethan England. Nineteenth-century evangelicals universally disapproved, and even the vast majority of Americans in the middle of that century thought theater attendance was sinful. Themes in the criticisms ranged from the immorality, laziness, and unrestrained passions of actors to the theater competing with the church in explaining reality.[35]

The art of acting itself, for some, was wrong. For J. C. Massee, acting was lying, a violation of the ninth commandment. To him, modern theater "sets forth lies in action to the detriment of public morals"; hypocrisy meant "play-acting." Riley, in answering positively to his own sermon question, "Is the Devil in Dramatic Art?" declared that actors were generally indifferent to virtue, the most "putrid" plays were the most popular, and the stage consorted with the degrading elements in society. Riley insisted that he would not attend the theater even for the best plays and best actors because it would set a bad example. Rader, no stranger to theatrics himself in his religious work, nonetheless argued that the theater could not be reformed because a purified theater would not be popular and would not make money. Gray, in a blend of eschatology and piety, recalled one pastor's remark "that he had never known a believer in the Lord's coming to be a frequenter of the theatre." For him and others, drama was not a priority in the end times.[36]

One fundamentalist who fought the stage most vigorously, given his location in New York City, was John Roach Straton. He battled Broadway, fearing that the "white-light" district would take the place of the old "red-light" district. "The theater is the devil's church," he insisted, a "covetous, mammon-worshiping, money-seeking institution." In fact, his main problem with theater was producing indecent plays to make money, "prostituted art on the altars of commercialism." He had other complaints: drama's appeal to the "lower instincts of the race," scantily clothed women, immorality and divorce associated with actors, and its pernicious effect on the young. Also, Sunday shows competed with church for attendance. In a less than veiled reference to Jewish theater owners, Straton further blamed the theater trust, "men who are utterly foreign to Christian ideals of life and conduct."[37]

In New York City Straton was not alone in his attacks. Earlier Rabbi Stephen S. Wise of New York had condemned the stage: "I indict the theaters as they are today. I don't care if every manager is a Jew—they are all heathens." Catholics and mainline Protestants also found common cause with evangelicals in efforts to close Sunday theaters and to censor objectionable elements.[38]

A series in the *Sunday School Times,* a testimonial of an actor who had left the theater to enter the ministry, poignantly delineated why "the Christian has no place on either side of the footlights." His personal experience, not the cries of a preacher, made his case compelling. From a Christian home, son of a minister, professing faith in Christ at twelve years old, the young man participated in school plays, went to a "better class of productions" at the theater, and became "devoted to Thespis." Dropping out of college, he acted on stage in New York City and for a few years in different companies traveled extensively. "My character suffered a slow disintegration. . . . I was morally and physically bankrupt," he confessed. "The Bible had been given up for good," and he developed a "hedonistic heart" and a philosophy of "esthetic materialism." Now, as an evangelical minister, he could condemn the evil, based on his past.[39]

For some fundamentalists the condemnation extended to drama in the church and in the Christian college; the dramatic form itself was inappropriate. Straton called "utter absurdity" the efforts to try and join the church with the theater; religious drama could be used by the theater people to get church people to countenance the theater. Some churches used drama to attract crowds, especially young people. Riley termed church involvement with theater as "constructing ante-rooms to perdition." Likewise, the *Moody Monthly,* despite the popularity of the theater among professing Christians, declared, "The theater and the Christian church have nothing in common." "If we partake of these amusements," the writer continued, "we are opening the gates through which some . . . may be swept into hell." Years later another writer in that periodical urged readers to seek an "abundant spiritual life," which comes "not by introducing the play in our churches." The simple gospel, not the dramatic play, brings great spiritual revivals, he concluded. The *Sunday School Times* went further: "There is only one thing for the consistent college to do—that college that wants to be four-square for Christ and his work. That is to eliminate dramatics from its calendar."[40]

Among fundamentalists in the interwar period, a small but significant debate focused on the role of culture and religion, particularly as it related to drama. Scofield and Gaebelein enjoyed the theater. Another strong proponent of "high" culture, ironically, was Bob Jones Sr., the son of an Alabama sharecropper. Jones, largely influenced by his wife, an upper-middle-class southerner, frequented art galleries and museums, traveled widely, and attended operas and concerts. For him, culture meant refinement: "The most refining influence that came to a human heart is Christianity. A man is inherently a gentleman who is a Christian. If you are not a gentleman at heart, there is something wrong with your religion."[41]

A newspaper reporter described Bob Jones Sr. as a "man who put a red carpet on the sawdust trail," meaning that high culture embellished the evangelistic emphasis. While Jones may not have had a natural inclination for Shakespeare or for Handel, he understood the benefit of refinement, even drama, for a Christian. Bob Jones Sr. encouraged his "preacher boys" to get involved in Shakespeare. A former dean of fine arts at the school concluded that Jones used culture to elevate fundamentalism to a higher level and also provided good public relations for the school, "status in the mind of the public," important since the school did not seek accreditation. In the early days culture was so emphasized that the school advertised in *Etude* as well as in Christian periodicals. Jones also wanted to counter the stereotype of the crude fundamentalist: "he must . . . have a greasy nose, dirty fingernails, baggy pants, and he mustn't shine his shoes or comb his hair." The school had never been embarrassed by drama or opera, Jones concluded, the way it had been at times by uneducated preachers. Furthermore in the spirit of the Apostle Paul's declaration, "I am made all things to all men, that I might by all means save some" (1 Cor. 9:22), Jones believed culture was "the method by which to put over the message of Christianity." High culture complemented evangelism; it broadened opportunities for witness.[42]

Soon after its founding, Bob Jones College developed something of a highbrow image. Bob Jones Jr. recalled that the school had a "profound effect on the way godly Christian people regard the arts. When the school was founded, it was an almost unheard-of thing for a fundamental Christian institution to give any attention to . . . drama." The school's emphasis on the arts countered "the impression that one who believes the Bible . . . must, perforce, be crude, uncultured, and ignorant," Jones continued. In the early years the college had only three majors: religion, music, and speech, two of the three in fine arts. In 1927, the school's first year, on Sunday afternoons a "Twilight Musicale" program blended inspirational music and drama. The next year, renamed "Vespers," the program also offered two biblical dramas. In 1930 the Bob Jones College Classic Players presented *The Merchant of Venice,* its first production. On the tenth anniversary of the Classic Players one critic praised their work as "amazingly fine in acting, setting, costuming and stage management." "It is strange," the critic continued, "that a notable theatrical achievement should spring from antipathy to the theater," given fundamentalist disdain for the stage. Guest artists also performed on campus, and by 1942 Bob Jones College staged its first grand opera, *Faust,* produced with guest artists from New York City's Metropolitan Opera.[43]

Bob Jones Jr. developed drama at his father's college in the 1930s, a role for which he was well suited. The product of an upper-middle-class southern upbringing, tastes shaped by a genteel grandmother, educated by private tutors while traveling with his evangelist father, he had a broad range of experiences, including travel overseas. When his father was in an evangelistic campaign, young Bob, alone in his hotel room, would perform his own plays, using sheets for curtains, according to advance man Willis Haymaker. By age twenty-one his theater work caught the eye of professionals; Warner Brothers offered him a screen test and contract, which he turned down. Later he studied Shakespeare for parts of two summers at Stratford-on-Avon in England. In 1935 and 1936 he was favorably received after performing at the national convention of the Shakespeare Association of America.[44]

After majoring in speech at Bob Jones College and minoring in history, Bob Jones Jr. joined the faculty in 1931 as a history instructor. In 1933 he completed a master's degree in history at the University of Pittsburgh, after taking some courses at the University of Chicago Divinity School. But drama was not forgotten. Jones did postgraduate work in drama and theater at Northwestern University, and around 1933 he developed *Curtain Calls,* his one-man show featuring about eight Shakespearean characters. He hired an agent and performed four weeks a year until 1945 at colleges, city auditoriums, and even Bible conferences such as Winona Lake. "These did more to build the school's name in educational circles than any other thing," reported *Christian Life* several years later.[45]

In 1934, at age twenty-three, Bob Jones Jr. became acting president of the college, in a position to give the school its cultural flavor. "I was pushing all the time for the drama," he recalled later, even being "sneaky" about it when his father was away preaching, not there to veto it. To him the School of Religion was most important, but he did not want fine arts "pushed aside." "My affection for Shakespeare, even his plays, is second only to my love for the Bible," he confessed. He found theological reading "deadly dull" and avoided it. One contemporary, Elizabeth Edwards, remembered that, for the early years of the school, drama was "all-consuming" for Bob Jr.; Bob Jones Sr. seemingly took care of the spiritual, evangelistic aspects of the school, and his son, the cultural part. Another colleague in fine arts recollected: "my perception is that Dr. Bob, Jr. paid lip service to the importance of religion, and I'm sure he was sincere in his own commitment to Christ. . . . whereas his heart was more in the culture." "Obsession is too strong a word," he added, but Jones was preoccupied with Shakespeare and later with opera. At the Cleveland, Tennessee, campus in the 1930s, Bob Jones Jr. designed the campus auditorium, one of the best in the region, with thirty curtains, an advanced lighting system, dressing rooms, a costume room, a greenroom (a lounge for performers before and after their appearances on stage), a scene shop, and a radio studio.[46]

Bob Jones Jr. defended his preference for drama; he believed the fundamentalist, with the decline of the classical stage and the rise of Hollywood movies, should not fear drama, considered impure by some because of links to the theater. Furthermore aesthetics raised questions of taste, not spiritual or moral issues, and tastes needed to be developed and educated. Performing Shakespeare, he argued, developed discipline, poise, and an appreciation for the best in literature and drama; it enhanced the aesthetic atmosphere of the school. The purpose was not to develop professional actors but to improve the performance of some ministerial students. "Our young ministerial students preach better sermons when they have been playing Shakespeare," he believed, and he felt that the "flow of language is more classic." Others observed the impact of the classical stage training on his preaching. Bob Jones Jr. had an unusual style, a blend of fundamentalist theology with a delivery that was eloquent, smooth, dramatic, expressive, and "modern," with its free, fluid structure.[47]

The Jones father-son combination proved a unique one for fundamentalism in the 1920s and 1930s. Bob Jones Sr. viewed culture mostly as personal refinement, and his son saw it as primarily the development of the arts. The father was the catalyst, providing a home and then a college for his son where artistic endeavors had his blessing. Bob Jones Sr. knew that his only child was artistic, and he sought to nurture that talent. In the process, Bob Jones Sr. legitimized this union of fundamentalism and drama.[48]

In a larger sense, the Joneses may have been participating in what historian Lawrence Levine has called the "sacralization" of culture. For much of the nineteenth century, Shakespeare was the most popular playwright with the American public and elites. Gradually after 1850, however, American theater divided into legitimate, or classical, theater for the upper class and popular theater for the masses. With this change in theater, "sacralization" of culture, Shakespeare shifted from popular to elite culture. Levine has argued that this process suggests a "collusion of religion and culture as elites in the late nineteenth century connected high arts with spirituality."[49]

For fundamentalists like the Joneses, performing Shakespeare involved questions of not only morals but also aesthetics and class. Bob Jones Jr., in a generation that had come of age in the 1920s and 1930s, particularly stressed high culture for the educational benefit and, in addition, its connection to upper-middle-class and elite society. He clearly believed that fundamentalism's image needed improving and that an association with high culture was one way to do it. With secular intellectual elites he shared a disdain for mass culture, but for both aesthetic and moral reasons, unusual for a fundamentalist.

Bob Jones Sr.'s acquiescence was not without misgivings. The decision to allow drama at the college was a major one and was made reluctantly. He determined that the school could perform only Shakespeare and classical works. He feared that an overemphasis on drama or any of the arts could divert attention from the spiritual mission of the school. Objectionable elements in Shakespeare had to be cut. "'Not even Shakespeare can cuss here,'" declared Bob Jones Jr. Bob Jones Sr. put more emphasis on the fine arts because of his son's involvement with the arts; once Bob Jones Jr. was in charge, he put even more emphasis on fine arts. "It used to kind of gnaw on him" that Bob Jones Jr. spent so much money on the arts, recalled Bob Jones III. The senior Jones felt like he "needed to keep the reins tight" on his son, or the younger man "would just go wild on the cultural expenditures around here," added Bob Jones III.[50]

Bob Jones Sr. feared adverse reactions for performing drama. A large portion of fundamentalists still looked down on drama of any kind—high culture like Shakespeare or the drama of popular culture. He sensed the danger that some people would consider the school liberal or unspiritual. He was right. Bob Jones Jr. remembered that in the early days "we were criticized more for presenting Shakespeare than for almost anything else." Because of its quality and since it had been studied in classrooms for centuries, Shakespeare seemed immune from criticism. "How wrong we were," Bob Jones Jr. recalled. One faculty member was fired for starting prayer meetings against the performing of Shakespeare at Bob Jones College. Karl E. Keefer, who entered as a freshman in 1938 and years later served as dean of fine arts, knew fellow students who believed involvement in Shakespeare was "almost heresy" or "going to the devil." Some of those students who were critical of drama, he figured, were "super-Fundamentalists" and from country churches. Moreover, the plays, opera, and artist series were not optional; students were required to attend. When parents complained, Bob Jones Sr. responded that any young people attending the school would go to the plays or would go home.[51]

The Joneses carefully defended their use of drama. They differentiated between commercial theater and drama; the former was evil, but the latter was fine if used properly. Again, they distinguished between a form, which was legitimate, and substance, which could be corrupt. Most fun damentalists did not make the distinction; theater was a generic term for any stage presentation—vaudeville, burlesque, monodrama, and Shakespeare—and all were worldly. Bob Jones Sr. answered that all good things are gifts of God, including fine arts. He tried to keep the school's use of drama in balance and was willing to live with criticism because he realized the new school needed "high culture" to distinguish it. Bob Jones Jr. argued that the college's Classic Players and opera helped not only the school but fundamentalism's image as well, important after the Scopes Trial.[52]

Opposition mounted from outside the school. Before a preaching engagement at Moody Church, Bob Jones Jr. performed his *Curtain Calls* in Evanston, Illinois. A Chicago paper carried the story about the presentation with a picture of him in costume. A deacon passed the picture around at a Moody Church board meeting, complained about the theater, and opposed having Bob Jones Jr. preach at the church. Pastor Harry A. Iron-side, without arguing, quoted briefly from familiar passages from Shake-speare, like Hamlet's "To be or not to be" soliloquy, and dismissed Jones's performance as innocuous. The board member was satisfied. Bob Jones Jr. had averted an embarrassment at the beginning of his ministry.[53]

Sharpest criticism of the use of drama at Bob Jones College came from President Buswell of Wheaton College. Buswell had kept drama off his campus, out of the curriculum, and out of extracurricular activities. Writ-ing in 1937, Buswell scolded "Christian parents who hire professionals to tell filthy stories to their children from the stage or from the screen!" For him the "only answer . . . is a complete and permanent boycott of all such places of amusement." Several years later he attacked Bob Jones Sr.: "Your own educational program is reeking with theatricals and grand opera which lead young people . . . into a worldly life of sin." Buswell, unlike the Joneses, did not distinguish the drama of popular culture from that of "high culture"; to him, both were corrupt.[54]

Bob Jones Sr. responded vigorously to Wheaton's criticism. "We have drama and get away with it," he retorted, because the college did not have intercollegiate football, which Wheaton did have, but which Bob Jones College dropped once it became a "spiritual handicap." Bob Jones Sr. complained later that Buswell was "always trying to make his conscience a guide for somebody else." "The drama in this school," Jones continued, "is just as sacred as a scientific laboratory." In 1949 he could only recall three students who came to the school and left with "stage inclinations." Factors other than drama fueled the tension between Jones and Buswell. Buswell resented the competition from Bob Jones College, begun in 1927, and considered Wheaton's academic standards to be higher; also Buswell, in the process of leaving the mainline Presbyterian church in the 1930s, probably considered himself at that time a more ardent separatist than Bob Jones Sr.[55]

Not everyone at Wheaton agreed with Buswell's starker view of drama. Frequently in the interwar years students complained in the campus news-paper about the narrow view of culture. If it is right to read Shakespeare for English class, one student asked, then why not perform it on stage? When a professor gave a reading of *Cyrano de Bergerac,* the student editor applauded the professor for providing what students wanted and asked for more of this sort of thing. Shortly afterward an editorial declared that the cultural level of Wheaton needed to be raised; it was deficient in comparison to eastern colleges. In 1931 a student editor raised the point that Wheaton needed more "high class lectures and musical entertainment on campus" without compromising its integrity; it needed to get away from its narrowness. By 1939, the year before Buswell's departure, the chafing had not stopped. The campus paper editorialized that a college education was more than studying; Wheaton students needed an education "along cultural lines." [56]

This debate over the application of popular cultural forms affected choices that fundamentalist young people made about college. Katherine Stenholm from Hendersonville, North Carolina, decided to attend Bob Jones College in the 1930s because it offered drama. An evangelist at her Grove Street Gospel Church recommended the school, and after seeing a yearbook, she "sensed a feeling of culture," something she had not felt after meeting students from Wheaton and Moody Bible Institute. People in her hometown, critical of drama, tried to dissuade her from attending, but she had shown a strong interest in drama from childhood. Ignoring their advice, she turned down a four-year scholarship to Wellesley to go to Bob Jones College. [57] Debate over drama clearly revealed disagreement among fundamentalists over cultural issues, at the grassroots level as well as among leaders. During the interwar years even greater controversies loomed as they grappled with secular culture in other forms.

4 Judging Popular Culture

      If fundamentalists generally condemned most elements of popular culture they had encountered, they responded more ambiguously to features unique to the 1920s and 1930s, from movies and radio to jazz and the new woman. Hollywood and film generated a complex reaction. Katherine Stenholm, who had enjoyed drama before entering Bob Jones College in 1936, also had reviewed movies for her hometown newspaper. In those days she "didn't think anything about going to the movies"; she had a pass and went to every movie that came to the local theater from 1931 to 1935. J. Gresham Machen enjoyed going to movies, spoke favorably about Charlie Chaplin, but remained quiet on the subject in print. Billy Graham recalled that as a child he and his family went to movies. If something objectionable appeared on the screen, his mother told him to close his eyes. Other fundamentalists obviously did not share their views. Liberal Protestants disagreed among themselves as well. Norman Vincent Peale served as a technical adviser to Warner Brothers and believed that a minister could feel very much at home in Hollywood. A few filmmakers were bad, but generally, he argued, they were "wholesome" and promoters of Americanism. On the other hand, several Methodist, Episcopal, and Presbyterian ministers in Brooklyn before World War I feared the theater more than the saloon and wanted theaters closed on Sundays and theater managers arrested.[1]

The moral battle over movies was much bigger than previous battles in the late nineteenth century over theater, vaudeville, and sports. Religious resistance, from both liberals and conservatives, developed for several reasons. First, there were moral concerns despite the apparently innocuous nature of most early films. The larger screen images made, for example, the lips or other body shots more sensuous and kissing more passionate, and movies encouraged questionable daydreams. In addition to the content and imagery on the screen, the behavior of the audience, especially young men and women, in the dark theater, troubled many. Also, movies were extremely popular and appealed to the masses more than theater, novels, and sports. Traditionalists feared that the new technological art form made modern values accessible to a mass audience. Middle-class people feared the effect on working-class Americans, particularly with movie houses located near saloons and brothels. The masses attended because movies were cheap. By the 1920s most Americans attended at least once a week; the most popular day at the box office was Sunday. In 1937 weekly movie attendance reached 88 million, more than three times the weekly attendance at all churches and synagogues. Not only was the content of the films objectionable, but the competition with churches was serious. "The movie industry," according to one scholar, "with its godlike stars and opulent exhibition palaces—resembling cathedrals right down to the massive organ—symbolized both the culture of consumption and a competing religious order."[2]

By the 1920s, movies had revolutionized the American world of entertainment, triumphing over vaudeville and theater. Beginning in the previous decade the feature-length film attracted middle- and working-class patrons. The movie trust, the Anglo-Saxon industry pioneers, lost out to the Jewish independent producers as the movie business shifted from New York to Hollywood with its studio star system. Jewish influence over the film industry, controlling an audience that was 90 percent nominally Christian, troubled many Protestants and Catholics.[3]

Mainline Protestantism in the early twentieth century responded to movies with efforts to suppress them. This Progressive Era strategy led city governments to close theaters on Sundays and regulate the exhibitors with inspections, higher fees, safety laws, and chaperoning of children. Movies were so profitable, however, that in places such as New York City they were exempted from regulations that affected theater and vaudeville. Also, self-censorship began in 1909 when the movie industry worked with the Federal Council of Churches, the YMCA, and other organizations to establish in 1915 the National Board of Review, which reviewed about 95 percent of the nation's films.[4]

In the second decade of the century filmmakers responded to those progressive pressures. D. W. Griffith, himself from a Methodist background, used Christian symbols in his films, and his epics featured conflicts between good and evil. Later, Cecil B. DeMille, the most influential director of the time, responded similarly, but he had less moral impact. In the 1920s his *Ten Commandments* and *King of Kings* represented a concession to religious critics, but as one scholar concluded, his most important cinematic ingredient, sex, was not sacrificed. His *Ten Commandments* put sex orgies in a biblical setting, and his other movies were a bit loose. His movies attracted both the middle class and the working class and were very profitable.[5]

Fundamentalist outrage against movies underscored a similar concern they shared with secular defenders of republican virtues; both feared that immorality threatened the family, the citizenry, and the state. Historian Jackson Lears characterized American republicans as those who feared excessive wealth and leisure and worried that immigrants as an urban mob might import European corruption to the American republic. He pointed out that republican proponents "urged men of property to cultivate sober responsibility and public duty." Such sentiments found expression in such disparate sources as McGuffey readers, college moral philosophy courses, and Thorstein Veblen's satire *The Theory of the Leisure Class*. Content analysis of movies in the 1920s revealed that themes of love, sex, and crime filled three-fourths of films. Research done around 1930 showed that movies taught young people about dating, sex, and racial stereotypes and brought dissatisfaction when they contrasted their lives with the glamour and excitement on the screen.[6]

"Movies are and always have been a revolutionary force," according to film critic Molly Haskell. The art form helped create consumerism and united it with popular culture. Movies generated desire, an impulse to please oneself through material gratification. Image became more vital than substance; both the department store owners and moviemakers focused on all-important packaging. In the early twentieth century Hollywood pursued women as moviegoers, as consumers, and films instructed them about love and marriage. Of course, morality became an issue as ideals of pleasure and luxury replaced Victorian notions of "hearth, sacrifice, and duty." Morals, art, and commerce often combined in controversial ways. "In the 1920s and early 1930s," Haskell concluded, "Hollywood was America's own Sodom and Gomorrah." [7]

To all those concerns fundamentalists could say "amen." Lamenting young people's knowledge of Hollywood, one complained: "they can tell you a great deal about Marlene Dietrich . . . but know little about Mary Magdalene." William H. Short, director of the Motion Picture Research Council in New York, pointed out in *Moody Monthly* that "A new educational system, rivaling the home, the school, and the church has grown up without our being aware of it." "The motion picture that sets in attractive perspective lust in all its forms and murder with all its mystery, involves its creators and directors in a wholesale slaughter of American youth," cried William Bell Riley. Two fundamentalists in Los Angeles joined the denunciations. R. A. Torrey, a pastor and evangelist, labeled movies as more vile and corrupt than any other institution, hurting young people and the old, but above restraints because of financial success. Hollywood, Bob Shuler feared, had supplanted public schools in educating American youth "in matters of life and daily conduct." James Oliver Buswell also continued his vigilance in rebuffing Twentieth Century Fox efforts to scout Wheaton College students. He called it a "disgrace if any of our graduates became moving picture actors or actresses. . . . Our young people are not open to the sinister influence of your scouts." At Wheaton students were socially restricted if they were caught attending movies. [8]

Fundamentalists consciously sensed that movies undermined republican virtue. Citing a report, the *Moody Monthly* claimed that there were almost as many movie theaters in 1920 as public schools and that Americans spent more hours at the movies than at school and church combined. The movies not only posed a moral threat to church and school and wasted capital, the report continued, but they were also "a crime against patriotism, a war against domestic virtue, and a sin against God." The editor warned parents that movies were "one of the most powerful and attractive forms of entertainment that art and science combined have ever invented." A few years later the same Christian magazine, citing Hollywood's violation of the Sabbath, its passionate advertising, and its avarice and calling it a "business whose every motive is rooted in evil," asked its readers: "Does that make for good citizenship?" Reverend William Evans, in the same publication more than a decade later, reiterated this theme: "The goal of religion and education is to produce character. The goal of movie entertainment is to produce thrills."[9]

The American home seemed especially vulnerable to Hollywood's influence. The *King's Business,* published by the Bible Institute of Los Angeles, cited the "record of the marital experiences" of actors as the biggest complaint against movies and indicated the movie world's example posed the greatest challenge to the "Christian ideal of marriage in America." The *Moody Monthly,* observing frequent divorces among the stars, called it a "business where professional whoredom seems to have acceptance." Addressing the issue of multiple marriages in Hollywood, Bob Jones Sr. condemned the city as "so rotten that it sends up a stench to the nostrils of the Almighty." Famous names in Hollywood, such as Fairbanks, Pickford, Garbo, Swanson, and Valentino, established a glamorous tone that included frequent divorces and sex in the movies. One film scholar concluded that Cecil B. DeMille as a director did strive to influence American manners and style with movies that "portrayed a world of luxury and leisure, of moral freedom." Little wonder that one evangelical critic of movies in 1927 concluded that by dulling the sensibilities of the masses, films produced "a corruption in politics, a laxity in morals and a lukewarmness in religion." To fundamentalists the republic was imperiled.[10]

Moral effrontery from the movie industry furnished grist for the fundamentalist attacks. Private lives of the stars interested but also alarmed the public, as with the famous "Fatty" Arbuckle scandal in 1921. Accused of a sadistic sexual assault, Arbuckle was eventually acquitted. His career was over, but not before the incident had confirmed the worst fears in the minds of religious critics of Hollywood, in both fundamentalist and mainline churches. Cries for censorship brought action in New York and five other states. The old National Board of Review had lost credibility by sanctioning D. W. Griffith's *Birth of a Nation,* so movie producers formed a trade association, the Motion Picture Producers and Distributors of America, to protect themselves. In a deft move, in 1922 they hired Will Hays, a Republican and respected Presbyterian layman, to head the organization.[11]

Hays banned two hundred people from the film industry for drinking, drugs, or immorality, had a list of do's and don'ts for Hollywood, and inserted moral clauses in actors' contracts. But his victories were essentially symbolic; few people were fooled by the film executives' use of this icon of middle-class Protestant respectability to shield themselves from criticism. Hays cleared Arbuckle and compromised between sex and traditional values in movies, permitting explicit sexuality in the closing years of the silent film era. In the 1920s he mainly protected movie executives from regulation. In 1925, mainly through the efforts of the Presbyterian Church, the Federal Motion Picture Council was formed and attacked Hays for paying the critics of Hollywood, literally putting them on the payroll. In 1930 *Christian Century,* a mainline Protestant voice, joined the council in faulting Hollywood's self-policing. These groups did not want censorship but sought more moral responsibility in films. But the arrival of sound in movies brought more sex and violence, and the depression meant more pressure to ignore moral concerns and make more money. Not surprisingly, in a 1933 study the council assailed the influence of movies, and the Catholic Church joined the fray by forming the Legion of Decency, which urged a ratings system and a boycott unless Hollywood reformed. In 1934 Hays installed a Production Code Administration to ensure a movie did not get a "C" rating, the worst. Hollywood's Jewish moviemakers worked with some of the Catholic proposals, although some Protestant liberals were skeptical of the Legion of Decency. In fact, Protestant liberals in the 1930s had an ambiguous view of movies, often critical but also sometimes praising questionable ones. Hays was not perfect from their standpoint, but neither were they consistent.[12]

Fundamentalists likewise contradicted themselves. In one sense they wanted censorship stronger than what Hays provided, but many also believed censorship would never work because movies were an essentially flawed medium. William Jennings Bryan counseled Hays to be tough with the Arbuckle incident. Although Arbuckle had been acquitted of any crime, Bryan argued that he should not be given another chance until he repented and changed his behavior. Bryan, a fellow Presbyterian layman, empathized with Hays's position between the movie business and the public, but the movie people, according to Bryan, were not sure about their moral standards. Bob Shuler and another Los Angeles pastor met Hays after his appointment and initially were convinced of his sincerity. Hays, with a meek demeanor and tears in his eyes, at one point asked the pastors for their prayers and reassured them that morality in the movies was his goal. Later, with movies remaining unchanged from his perspective, Shuler continued to attack them as well as the conduct of the stars. He concluded that Hays was being used by movie executives to head off protests. Shuler called Charlie Chaplin a "moral pervert" and chided Hays for protecting him. Mordecai Ham derided Hays as a "hired wet nurse and a smokescreen for the depravity of the motion pictures."[13]

Curiously, some fundamentalists agreed with Hays about the futility of censorship. Hays argued it was ineffective, un-American, and unnecessary because Hollywood would outgrow through competition its "low level" of films. Some of the religious critics despaired of censorship for different reasons. The *King's Business,* quoting a secular paper, pressed the point that "The movie is dirty because it is a low order of entertainment . . . requiring merely action to carry its message. . . . But to clean up the movies is like going at the leopard with Kalsomine." Likewise, the *Sunday School Times* concluded that movies could not be "cleansed" because "such fundamental factors of unworthiness [are] involved,—in plain words sin,—that their cleansing is out of the question." Movies made so much money, and sex in movies helped make them profitable, that the industry remained above the courts and censorship, critics continued to argue. William Bell Riley noted that the Chicago Censorship Board in 788 films found 757 scenes of nudity and 1,811 scenes of assault with weapons. Fundamentalists also were not hopeful for the success of the Catholic Church's Legion of Decency campaign.[14]

The question of Hollywood movies aside, fundamentalists also had to confront another controversial issue: should they use the motion picture medium to further the kingdom of Christ? Some said absolutely not. R. A. Torrey, though willing "to adapt the . . . method of argument to the thinking of our own day," found it unnecessary for his Los Angeles church to resort to movies or other "sensational features" to attract crowds. Preaching Christ, Torrey continued, attracts the audience; he never showed a movie in his church. *Moody Monthly* in 1920 condemned as "sacrilegious" a motion picture version of the Bible. It belonged to the realm of the "prince of darkness," and the "greatest evil" it posed was the threat to the preaching of God's word, its editor concluded. On the use of films the

King's Business declared that "when the church resorts to them as a means of aiding the work of our Lord we can only bow our heads in shame."[15]

Charles G. Trumbull and the *Sunday School Times* had the most torturous film policy, reflective of fundamentalist ambiguity about the technology. "There is distressing evidence of the readiness of churches and ministers to use theatrical motion picture films and try to 'redeem' that which cannot be redeemed because of its essential antagonism to the cross of Christ," complained the editor. "What a strange, regrettable yoking up of the church and the world this is!" he added. Clarifying the periodical's position a week later, he concluded that "there is a legitimate use of motion pictures of the right sort, and at the right time, by the church." Films could be utilized to promote missions and to instruct, but the *Sunday School Times* issued these guidelines: dramatic motion pictures with professional actors and actresses should be "barred . . . by the church under all circumstances"; "natural life motion pictures," those depicting real life, not re-creations for film, could be used by the church; only religious motion pictures were appropriate for Sunday use; and "the church may properly make use of secular natural motion picture films, on weekdays, as an incidental part of its work in the field of social or educational life." The paper even advertised those films that fit its criteria.[16]

Other fundamentalists did not agonize over the issue as did Trumbull. Endorsement of movies had occurred around the turn of the century when Protestants often sponsored Lyman H. Howie, a popular movie exhibitor, although they had condemned urban commercial entertainment. On the summer Chautauqua circuit, in small towns, churches, and the YMCAs, his films with moral but not overtly religious subjects were commended. On the eve of World War I, movies with moral lessons and educational value appeared. Churches and Sunday schools showed biblical films; Moody Bible Institute attracted people to its revival meetings with movies. In the 1920s churches used films to attract Sunday evening audiences, and by 1923 approximately 15,000 church schools and clubs relied on motion pictures in their work. Charles M. Sheldon, editor of *Christian Herald* and author of the best-seller *In His Steps,* sensed as he worked on a film version of the book that "The film people are already beginning to see the handwriting on the screen and are beginning to look around for religious subjects." Optimistic in 1922 about the public's film preferences, he continued: "It is a good sign of the general public that it is growing tired of the sex and self pictures." Bryan, also hopeful, viewed the motion picture as neither moral nor immoral, but only a means, depending on its use. Film, he thought, could be valuable for the "propagation of moral truths." "I expect to see the legitimate use of the moving picture increase," Bryan wrote in 1923, "and the demoralizing use of the moving picture decrease."[17]

Fundamentalist application of film abounded in the interwar period. Paul Rader had three silent films produced covering his Chicago Gospel Tabernacle activities in 1928, his family, and, ever the dramatist, his deathbed and funeral. Rader boasted about using modern methods to get the gospel out. Years later, in his early eighties and still dignified, Riley used film to preach on a favorite topic, the Second Coming. Religious movies were shown at the Winona Lake Bible Conference. Homer Rodeheaver, with his promoter's instincts, tried to persuade Billy Sunday in 1931 to film a series of sermons as a good way to get the gospel out, but also as a steady source of income. Wheaton College by the late 1930s owned sound and silent pictures and showed them at house parties and literary society meetings; professors there used motion pictures widely in the classrooms. President Buswell instructed his recruiters or field men, over their opposition, to continue using moving pictures instead of slides in presentations to young people's groups and churches. Bob Jones College proudly advertised: "We have our own picture show, and, once a week, a carefully censored picture, either humorous or of an uplifting, character building kind."[18]

Probably no one matched the enthusiasm of Bob Jones Sr. for film. Calling the moving picture machine the "most thrilling invention in the world," he was perhaps the first to use silent film as a tool for mass evangelism. Early in 1925, with financial support from business, he wrote and produced a "dramatized sermon film," *The Unbeatable Game,* in which he starred. Cast members included members of his evangelistic organization and actors from the Philadelphia area, where it was shot on location. It premiered May 11 in Philadelphia's Lyric Theatre, but not without controversy. The Pennsylvania Board of Motion Picture Censors cut 1,500 feet of the film. Jones's depictions on screen of the destructive effects of sin apparently had gone too far: venereal disease, illegitimate children, and adultery. An angry Jones spoke to the audience before the premiere; he criticized the censors for "mutilating" the film and defended the work because it showed one could not sin and get away with it. *The Unbeatable Game* was "intensely moral," he told the crowd, and had been approved by ministers across the country. He offered a refund to anyone who wanted one.[19]

Reviews of Jones's movie revealed this medium's shortcomings as an evangelistic tool. Critics praised the photography as "picturesque and appealing" and noted that some of the acting was adequate. "But it wasn't up to Hollywood" standards, Jones confessed. "They're smarter than we are." Although the film had a clear lesson, critics doubted if it had any amusement or entertainment value. One reviewer judged that teaching and drama were an awkward mix and that the "screen is a difficult medium for him to work with." From a technical standpoint, the censorship hurt the continuity of the film—there were too many close-ups of Bob Jones.[20]

Perhaps fundamentalists had mixed feelings about film. Although it could raise questions about morality and art, it was primarily a business. Movies played a role in reinforcing the consumer society, which many fundamentalists found attractive. As the urban working class and middle class pursued leisure, pleasure, and romance, motion pictures after World War I visualized the self-indulgence and self-fulfillment offered by the marketplace. While the films of DeMille, for example, raised eyebrows and made money, they also, according to William Romanowski, blended the "consumer lifestyle and the new morality of urban culture."[21]

▪

The radio, a new medium in the 1920s, also presented challenges and opportunities for fundamentalists. Critical to their adaptation to the consumer society, radio had significance as well for the threats of popular culture. "Should we as Christians listen to the vaudeville performances, the plays . . . that are sent out over the radio when we would not give our presence to them in person?" a "radio fan" inquired of the *Sunday School Times*. The columnist responded with a general admonition for purity, but with no specific rule for radio. Some feared that radio posed a threat to churches, especially in rural areas, with the temptation for listeners to substitute "radio worship" for attendance in church.[22]

Those doubts about radio were exceptions; generally fundamentalists embraced it eagerly with little of the anguish that had accompanied their attitudes about film. The reasons were apparent. Many believed it would increase interest in religion. One scholar labeled radio as "Protestantism's dream medium of advertising" because it was direct, it was private, and it worked with the home. Although liberal Protestants generally did not fare well on the radio with a noncontroversial or bland message, conservatives with attacks on society and appeals for salvation cultivated an audience, often a virtual paying "sponsor." Also, much of the programming in the 1920s—classical music, political addresses, and news, no commercials—posed little moral concern. Film with its powerful visual impact often tempted viewers, Christians believed, to surrender to the "lust of the eyes." The sound of radio seemed instead to stimulate the imagination in innocent ways.[23]

In 1925 churches owned 63 of the 600 stations operating in the United States, and many fundamentalists owned their own stations. In 1931 the "*Sunday School Times* Radio Directory" listed "sound and scriptural" broadcasts on 159 stations. Even in the 1930s, after radio had become a source of mass entertainment with commercial success, "gospel" programs remained popular. A 1932 survey by the *Kansas City Star* revealed that Walter L. Wilson's *Morning Bible Hour* finished first, just ahead of *Amos and Andy.* Apparently many listeners shared the feelings of a correspondent to the *Moody Monthly,* a Jewish woman who had converted to Christianity: "In my great loneliness . . . the radio means more to me than I can tell you. . . . I think there must be many of God's bewildered and oppressed children situated like myself in peculiar circumstances where WMBI seems as the voice of God."[24]

Although film seemed to confront the spirituality of many believers, radio fostered it. One pastor declared radio "the most amazing discovery of modern times . . . suggestive of deeper truths, religious lessons." Film contributed to the decline of the family and home, but radio built them up, he argued. Small towns and rural areas now could benefit from cultural and religious opportunities that had been available mainly in the cities. Therefore, he concluded, the medium was an "important factor in the development of our domestic and social life." Radio waves for communication reflected the nature of prayer and, he added, teach "the importance of right relations as to the invisible." Ralph E. Stewart of Moody Bible Institute's Radio Department celebrated the "romance" of radio, the "modern altar" in the home. Unlike the commercial stations, WMBI carried no advertising and provided religious programming for the home—Bible teaching and preaching, sacred music, and stories. "Let the saints welcome these modern discoveries and inventions, for unholy as the use of some of them now are," the editor of the *Moody Monthly* exclaimed, not only do they have usefulness, but the human achievement of such great marvels makes it much easier to believe the miracles accompanying the Second Coming.[25]

Radio brought another element of popular culture into the home that offended conservative Christians—jazz. For some it raised questions about the appropriateness of radio. "We hate jazz," one reader wrote the *Sunday School Times,* "and often it is hard to get much else but that" on the radio. Born in late-nineteenth-century New Orleans as a gimmick to attract people to the red-light district, jazz—the word itself meant sexual intercourse, perhaps a black slang expression—with its improvisation, polyrhythms, and syncopation evident in the radio music of the 1920s, did little to commend it to traditionalists. This new music, a blend of African and European elements, also encouraged new dances among African American and white young people. Jazz ranked near the top of the list as a cultural threat.[26]

Fundamentalists in the Jazz Age had little sympathy for its music. "I consider it the most hellish, insidious robber of the morals of our youth that has been invented by Satan," one Christian musician declared. Students in a clubroom at Bob Jones College happened to play "Hallelujah! I'm a Bum," a syncopated parody of "Revive Us Again," on a Victrola when Bob Jones Sr. happened to walk by. The evangelist took the record, and later in the chapel service he broke it over his knee, stepped on it, and then preached against the irreverent spirit of the day. "That's the Slimy Serpent tramping on human character," he thundered. In 1931 the faculty passed resolutions against the playing of jazz over the clubroom radio, and college rules dictated that twenty-five demerits be given for listening to music considered jazz by the head of the music department.[27]

As a reflection of the modern temper, conservative Christians attacked jazz for nurturing the irrational and uncertain elements of life. To them, chaos reigned in labor-industrial relations, in politics, in religion, and in philosophy, and the radio bombarded the home with what one writer termed "the worst form of musical chaos," "the symptom of a chaotic mental and moral condition." Just as modernists delved into the darker side of human life, this modern music called jazz, to them, betrayed a primitive, savage, and heathen foundation. The blend of syncopation or rhythm and tonal dissonance struck them as unnatural. To J. C. Massee, jazz, with its stress on the traditionally unemphasized beat, produced a "bump, a hump, and a thump" and a confusion similar to scrambling eggs. Massee believed that people who performed this "medley of demons" were "irrational animals, living . . . on passion, on desire." Charles G. Trumbull perceived in jazz "an abandonment and defiance of the principles that make for beauty and truth"; he saw it as an appeal "to the worst in human nature and abandoning all semblance of control."[28]

They also scorned jazz because of questions of class and taste. The *Moody Monthly* decried the corruption in music as part of the degeneracy in manners and morals. Religious songbooks of the early twentieth century, the editor believed, reflected the effects of modern music, and he urged readers to "cultivate a taste for better things" because jazz in sacred music "lowers the spiritual tone of public worship." The Bob Jones College rulebook for the 1930s boldly declared: "Bob Jones College endorses high class music. Students who persist in inflicting any other type music on the institution will be dealt with by the faculty committee." Wheaton College consciously strove to have first-class religious programs in order to compete with the secular world for an audience. That meant, of course, using music of the highest quality.[29]

As with other aspects of the modern world, jazz made inroads into the evangelical culture that spurned it. Paul Rader seemed least afraid of being touched by it. To him, musical innovation meant a greater opportunity to reach his young people, whom he termed "youth aflame," not "flaming youth." His music director pointed out that the Salvation Army broke down the barrier to brass, drums, and strings in the church. A church band or orchestra, he continued, could "harness" young people for the church and steer them from jazz bands and other secular entertainment. Homer Rodeheaver's trombone playing for Billy Sunday or at the Winona Lake Bible Conference struck some as too "jazzy."[30]

Complaints about the influence of jazz on religious music indicated that it had made an impact. One Methodist protested that traditional gospel songs such as "At the Cross" and "Beulah Land" were "permeated with jazz." Upon hearing about a pastor who introduced a jazz band into his services, the editor of the *King's Business,* Keith L. Brooks, exclaimed "Lord, help the man! . . . He who attempts to fight the devil with his own weapons will certainly find him an overmatch." [31]

An area of great ambiguity was the gospel song, which sometimes had syncopation and therefore was, for some, too close to jazz. One gospel song publisher, Herbert G. Tovey, warned that "The world of jazz is creeping into our Gospel song life." He suggested that if a song "goes with a swing and has a little jazz," people will like it. For him, the danger was placing melody above lyrics, especially when the melody was drawn from popular hits. Young people, he believed, were particularly vulnerable to jazz's influence: "once in control . . . it will cheat the young people of our churches out of the training rightly due them, and they will grow up with a light and cheap conception of 'Psalms and hymns and spiritual songs.'" [32]

▪

In the interwar period, concerns about popular culture culminated in the debate about the role of women in American society. Women, critical to the consumer culture, were also important to leisure changes in the 1920s, the swelling therapeutic culture. The new woman of the 1920s threatened the Victorian domestic ideal. The flapper image evoked associations with sexual promiscuity, consumerism, love of fashion and makeup, attraction to romance novels, and other menacing traits. Culprits, according to William E. Biederwolf, were the "awful rush of business and commercialism and this awful pleasure craze that is sweeping the land." The home was being wrecked because "Religion is being pushed aside and its place supplied with pleasure, business and recreation," Reverend D. W. Askew lamented. Charles Blanchard also decried the influences of industrialism, wealth, and "sensuous pleasures" in ruining the home. Another fundamentalist observed that women were abandoning the home because of a "consuming desire for life's luxuries." It was perhaps not coincidental that fundamentalism became most militant at a revolutionary time in manners and morals. Facets of mass culture—movies, theater, novels, magazines, newspapers, and other amusements—often presented young women in ways that challenged traditional notions about gender. Again conservative Christians responded ambivalently.[33]

As the world became more decadent, the home stood as a stark counterpoint. Historian Ted Ownby has concluded that southern evangelicals strove to keep from their homes masculine forms of recreation that "threatened the idealized purity of women." "The evangelical home," he continued, "was a sacred institution, standing as a place without sin in contrast to the world outside the home and church." Historian Betty DeBerg, also observing the early twentieth century, argued that as the "domestic" became "sacred," the home supplanted the church in fundamentalist literature "as the primary location of religious meaning and as the cornerstone of Christian civilization."[34]

"A home should be a little church," Mordecai Ham exhorted to a Charlotte, North Carolina, audience, a place for prayer, correction, and amusement. A. C. Dixon announced that "Nothing on earth exceeds in sacredness the sanctity of the home life." In a Chautauqua lecture Bob Jones Sr. cited the "home peril" as one of America's most serious dangers. John Roach Straton called the "right home life, the mainstay of the republic." For him, a mother, father, and children around the fireplace having prayer and reading the Bible was the strength of the republic, not the army or navy. Another observer concluded that the home was no less than "the backbone of civilization," and it, not modern material possessions, produced character. "When womanhood falls, the home falls," one letter to the *Moody Monthly* asserted, and "When the home falls, the government falls with it."[35]

One touchstone of fundamentalist anxiety about home and women was the emergence in the 1920s of what one scholar has called the "shocking model of the new feminism," the flapper, "with her bobbed hair, rolled stockings, cigarettes, lipstick, and sensuous dancing." Again popular culture shared the blame. The "sex idea," offered John Roach Straton, was "overemphasized in our modern life anyway," in movies, theater, magazines, novels, and women's dress. The editor of the *Moody Monthly* likewise cited those factors for contributing to the "sex foulness of our day." Such rhetoric, linking and condemning popular amusements, women's behavior, and the new morality, pervaded fundamentalist sermons and periodicals after 1910.[36]

Postwar America had experienced some real changes in morals, but calling it a sexual revolution might be overstating it. The Victorian moral code, thanks to fundamentalists and other middle-class Americans, remained strong. In small towns and big towns before World War I, authorities arrested women for smoking in public, using profanity, wearing shorts or slacks, or not wearing corsets. Within a decade such prosecutions had stopped. In 1919 skirts were only six inches above the ground, and by 1927 they had reached the knee. "Some of us older ones never saw above the shoe-top of even our mothers," one Christian educator noted. "Now, what with above-the-knee skirts, bathing-beauty contests, one piece bathing suits . . . the female form divine is clad in little more than the circumambient atmosphere." He lamented, "Everywhere you go, everywhere you read, everywhere you look, there is the ever protrusive, everlasting sex-appeal. You see it on the billboards . . . in the Sunday supplements . . . in the advertisements . . . in the magazines—low class and high—everywhere . . .—sex, sex, sex!" Another decried the "bobbed haired, painted faced, varnish lipped, step-ladder-heeled, knicker-clad, cigarette-smoking, card-playing jazz flapper" and commented that if Christianity could not save women from the "popular, fashionable sins of the world," it was powerless. Fundamentalists were not the only ones to notice and complain. Columnist Walter Lippman and liberal Protestant Harry Emerson Fosdick bemoaned America's apparent absorption with sex.[37]

For Bob Jones Sr., the concern over women's changing role was a major theme of his messages during the period. "The modern problem is becoming a woman problem," he declared, and "as far as world consequences are concerned the sin of woman is worse than the sin of man." He added, "The love of pleasure stabs dead the mother instinct." A common ploy, which Jones utilized, was to blame women for men's moral failures. He argued that the serious problem was women's dress: "It tempts a man constantly." He blamed both the war and women for bestial behavior in men. Straton likewise believed women's dress styles provoked men to think about sex, their dress "a living invitation to lust." "Pleasure-seeking" put man on the animal level, Riley contended, "one with the brutes." Particularly alarming was the realization that Christian women were following the fashion of prostitutes and that "flapper mothers" along with professional men and women had accepted the "new morality." "Stupifying to the moral sense," James M. Gray called it.[38]

One Nebraska pastor created a stir among *Moody Monthly* readers by insisting in an article that Paul's statement in 1 Corinthians 11:15, "if a woman have long hair it is a glory to her," was not of "secondary importance." The editor defended the pastor and also was alarmed that "professedly Christian women, church members and Sunday-school teachers, had so little respect for the Scriptures as to bob their hair." Short hair for women served as one more mark in the moral decline since the war: "The slump has been even more marked in women than in men. Some of them seem to wish to ape men, their dress, their amusements, their manners," he sadly concluded. In the 1920s the Wheaton campus divided on the issue of bobbed hair. An editorial in the campus paper struck an uncharacteristically moderate tone for fundamentalists. It cautioned against condemning women with bobbed hair. "Do the sheers sever her religion?" the editor queried and suggested the issue may be one of taste, with short hair acceptable on some and not on others.[39]

If the flapper phenomenon posed a serious social threat, then feminism presented a most grim ideological challenge. The movement for women's rights confronted the Victorian marriage ideal, which for fundamentalists was the biblical ideal. No longer was the husband head of the home and the wife restricted to her sphere, the care of home and children and taming the man; during the interwar period romantic love and companionship increasingly defined modern marriage. A rising divorce rate indicated an unwillingness of women to tolerate unhappy marriages. A steady increase in working women made divorce possible through financial independence. After the attainment of suffrage in 1920, feminism as a movement declined; however, extremists in the cause began pushing in the 1920s for an equal rights amendment. Fundamentalists took the feminist effort seriously.[40]

By a margin of ten to one, fundamentalists had opposed suffrage, citing arguments about separate roles for the sexes. For some it was against nature, contrary to God's order and scripture. The Wheaton College campus paper pointed out that women did not need to vote when they could mold voters. "New freedom and new feminism! that's the answer," thundered

Bob Jones Sr. "And as the vote spreads and more women are emancipated there's going to be a further and further slackening of old bonds and conventions. That means license, more divorces and fewer marriages, free thinking and free love. It's nauseating." Bryan and Sunday had favored suffrage, as had some voices at Wheaton. Women must not live only through their husbands and children, one writer on campus conceded, and one female student criticized politicians for being "blinded by their fears." Calling husband and wife "co-workers," she believed women had a right to demand the vote, so that they could fight the evils in the world.[41]

There was little room, however, for mixed feelings about the larger issue, feminism, between the wars. "What a calamity has thus fallen upon our generation!" mourned James M. Gray about women striving for equality and "undervaluing marriage." Again linking it to flapper-like behavior, Charles G. Trumbull declared "Feminism . . . shows us woman insisting upon taking her place in any and every vocation, responsibility, and activity of man, and thus it is a plain expression of the lawlessness of humanity today in revolt against God." God made man and woman distinct "in their responsibilities and mutual relationship. Woman cannot take over man's responsibilities . . . without defying God." Revealing the influence of modern drama, Straton warned that America needed women who knew "more about their Bibles than about Ibsen." "In this day and time," commented another writer, "the feminism cult has come to such a pass that some women . . . say their prayers to 'mother and father God.'" The idea of man as head of the house, he added, is "hooted and jeered by some unmarried and unmarriageable he-women" who tell husbands, Paul, and God Almighty "where they get off." Mel Trotter, whose wife left him in the 1920s but whose rescue mission ministry continued, called worldly women "frizzleheaded dunces" and charged that the "American woman pities her sister who has six children." Evangelist John R. Rice capsuled many fundamentalist objections to feminism that sprang from popular culture with his "classic" book *Bobbed Hair, Bossy Wives and Women Preachers.*[42]

Two books in the late 1920s further stirred debate about women and sexual behavior. Margaret Mead's *Coming of Age in Samoa* presented a primitive culture in which natives enjoyed guiltless sexual freedom, and Judge Ben Lindsey in *Companionate Marriage* argued that couples should live together before marriage, enjoy sex, and separate by mutual consent, without alimony, unless children were involved. Lindsey's book, though it exaggerated the extent of the sexual revolution, introduced an idea into the culture that encountered fierce opposition, and not just from fundamentalists. It touched off debates about birth control and the purpose of marriage. Christians and non-Christians worried about divorce. By the late 1920s one out of six marriages ended in divorce, up from one out of seventeen in 1890. Companionate marriage, many feared, would make the trend worse.[43]

Legalization of birth control information and devices in many states, and the acceptance of the practice by the middle class, made such a moral upheaval possible. Margaret Sanger in her book *Happiness in Marriage*, published in 1926, emphasized sex for pleasure, not for procreation, and birth control made that possible. Couples could also have fewer children for economic reasons. "When the primeval lust of the beast is the basis of union, the divorce mill is sure of its grist," warned William Bell Riley. He called birth control "a menace to humanity." James O. Buswell advised young ministers not to practice birth control. "Have a normal godly home," or your testimony may suffer. James M. Gray showed solidarity with the pope in opposing birth control by quoting his encyclical on the subject.[44]

Fundamentalists denounced another consequence of birth control—childless marriages. They believed that one important cause of divorce was the lack of children. Biblical teaching, for them, dictated that children were the prime purpose of marriage, and the happiness of the husband and wife was only secondary. J. C. Massee proclaimed that the basis of marriage is love, not lust, and the object of marriage is children. "Pleasure without children" he called "legalized concubinage" and a "blight" on society. Bob Jones Sr. joined the condemnation of childless marriages and small families, "husbands and wives who hellishly limit the size of their families because they are too damnably mean and selfish to raise children." He blamed men for being too concerned about money and success.[45]

Florence Nye Whitwell, a wife, college graduate, and fundamentalist, wrote about how shocking the idea of companionate marriage appeared. As she discussed it with other professional women, "it seemed unreal and

fantastic" how casually these women presented it and how biblical marriage seemed to some like "slavery." One "intellectual" Christian woman,
however, helped her put it in perspective by telling her and a "modern"
female acquaintance that the modern woman, in contrast to the Victorian
one, was "a poor, deluded dupe." "'The mid-Victorian,'" the woman
continued, "placed a value on herself. . . . She either received for the gift
of her person a husband, a home, a place in society . . . or if she chose the
primrose path, she received . . . jewels, often! . . . You moderns give your-
self and get nothing." Companionate marriage, this woman with an "old-
fashioned Bible outlook" concluded, was not a fair exchange.[46]

One more feature of feminism, prompted by the flapper, was the question of homosexuality. The flapper persona troubled fundamentalists
because it threatened gender distinctions with its mannish hair, boyish
figure, and cigarette smoking. But it was more than androgyny. "The
'modern woman' is masculine, bossy, and wants to run things," complained Bob Jones Sr. Lesbianism came up three times as an issue in a
woman's advice column in the *Sunday School Times* during the interwar
period, albeit in an oblique Victorian manner. Three girls wrote, troubled
about their love for other girls. One object of affection was a "yielded"
Christian and a Bible institute student. "I have never had much sympathy
for the girl who had a 'case' on another girl," answered "Mother Ruth,"
and she advised her to not let this friendship keep her from having other
friends. Another case proved more complex. A young woman confided
that there was a "strong physical attraction" between her and a minister's
daughter, and they "jokingly call each other 'husband and wife.'" The
problem: her friend did not have a deep spiritual life and refused to go to
prayer meeting with her. What really troubled her was that her friend delighted in popular amusements: "She likes to dance . . . and she enjoys
'a good movie.'" "Mother Ruth" cautioned her about the strong physical
attraction, stating "You dare not be under bondage to the flesh," and
advised that she "be bold for the Lord, and take a firm and determined
stand" in confronting her friend, prayerfully.[47]

Concerns about class permeated the gender problem for fundamentalists, as evidenced by their rhetoric. Upper-class or society women were
a favorite target, blamed for corrupting middle-class women. Popular
amusements, specifically the theater, were more of a temptation for upper-

class women than middle-class ones, Riley argued. He also blamed them, the "cultured and rich" in America, for trying to escape the "curse of conception" and the depression contributed to that attitude shifting to the middle class when economic factors meant few children. Straton called the declining birthrate among the well-to-do an "avoidance of sacred duty." Instead of women with children there were, he sarcastically pointed out, "all up and down our streets . . . women with puny little dogs at the ends of strings."[48]

Most of the women's issues of the interwar era—popular culture, sexual mores, birth control, and the flapper—were middle-class concerns, but the sexual freedom of the working class also affected them. One writer noted that in newspapers, magazines, and novels there was "Profanity everywhere," not just in the lower-class characters but even in "college-bred men and women." Some sympathized with the businesswoman of the 1920s, who often had to choose between home and a career. Women, one editor noted, sometimes use business as a means to meet a husband. Those who married and worked, and between 1900 and 1930 the number of wives working outside the home tripled, increasingly expected more of marriage—"equality," a "fifty-fifty basis in the financial arrangement," and companionship. Her personal freedom, income, and accomplishments made marriage difficult, he concluded. Bessie Morris Johnson ministered, through the Chicago Gospel Tabernacle, to young businesswomen in that city and tried to keep them from "running around the streets, indecently dressed, and spending their time in shows." She found them hard to evangelize with their "spirit of freedom and independence" and their "love of clothes." Johnson regarded them as "sophisticated and developed," with a "spirit of self-sufficiency and confidence."[49]

Although fundamentalists denounced the morals of lower-class women, an urban mix of young working-class, immigrant, and poor white women, some like Straton in New York City, sympathized with them. "I stood one morning at the end of Brooklyn Bridge, watching the working girls crossing over. . . . Here they came . . . a somewhat dreary procession. . . . My heart went out to them with a great compassion. Never before [has] . . . this great army of working girls, had such burdens to bear as they have today," Straton despaired. Two problems faced them particularly, he believed: their need to leave home and find work in factories and their poverty, which tempted them to fall into immorality. A prostitute, he charged, made four times more than a woman working in a department store.[50]

Clearly, conservative evangelicals sensed a problem with the modern woman. But their remedy was rife with contradictions, equivocating between elevating women, even to the point of participating in evangelical ministries, while simultaneously diminishing their public role. Not only did this ambivalence or tension characterize fundamentalism as a whole, but it also resided in the attitudes of individual fundamentalist leaders. Christianity puts women on a "pedestal of privilege and ease," Riley preached to a female audience. Later he wrote that Christianity is women's Magna Carta; it liberates and elevates women unlike other religions. He also quoted Galatians 3:28 where Paul declared, "In Christ Jesus there is neither male nor female." Ida M. Hudson, "Mother Ruth," of the *Sunday School Times* advice column, shared this view. "Don't have any foolish notions about suffrage and the woman question of the day," she responded to a reader troubled about God's treatment of women, "for, my dear, if woman is not careful today she will rob herself of all the high glory that has been hers through the years under Christian civilization. . . . Let us be careful that we do not stray from this wonderful and loving God." Reaffirming the Victorian ideal of motherhood, fundamentalists often praised their godly mothers and in that way glorified women. The exaltation of the home in their rhetoric also implied similar feelings of praise for women, even if they relegated women to a specific place.[51]

Although the fundamentalists saw separate spheres for the sexes after World War I, one scholar has concluded that "the lines were far more fluid than the image of separate spheres implies." Historians have missed the fact that "Fundamentalism was comparatively open to women in public ministry," he continued, because they looked at rhetoric, not deeds, and have focused on men, not the women of the movement. Men and women shared participation in evangelism, missions, music, writing, and Christian education and as Bible teachers and college and Bible institute professors. Their outreach extended beyond the nineteenth-century urban missions work.[52]

Evidence of prominent female fundamentalist ministries abounds. *Literary Digest* in 1926 featured the Reverend Patty Horn, pastor of a Disciples of Christ church in Promise City, Iowa. Though she wore a shingled bob and used lipstick and powder, she was not, in the eyes of one observer, a "flapper pastor," not a "hard-shelled, man-hating old maid," and she did not smoke, drink, swear, listen to jazz, or engage in petting or joyriding. Likewise, some fundamentalist women had a seriousness of purpose, encouraged by their male counterparts. J. C. Massee lauded women as effective "soul winners"; they not only had "certain graces and charms" but also had the leisure time in which to practice them. William Bell Riley urged pastors to work with women leaders because in the New Testament "women played no inconspicuous part," and it was "inconceivable, therefore, that women's work should be either disregarded or minimized in the Church of God." His Northwestern Schools enrolled students with irregular academic backgrounds and kept costs low, which attracted working-class and lower-middle-class female students, training them to be pastors' wives, church secretaries, and missionaries, but also pastors and evangelists. Northwestern Schools often encouraged women to be ministers and evangelists. The most famous alumnae ministers were Alma Reiber and Irene Murray, who as preacher and song leader, respectively, toured the upper Midwest after 1910 for thirty years. As late as 1937 Riley's *Pilot* advertised Reiber and Murray as "school-sponsored evangelists." Furthermore, all nine Northwestern graduates in eastern Kentucky in the 1930s and 1940s were women involved in home missions.[53]

The *Moody Monthly* sanctioned female ministries as well. Paul's admonition in 1 Corinthians 14:34 for "women to keep silence in the churches" was not a "general repression of the proper exercise of the spiritual gifts of women." Rather, "It was only improper and indecorous acts that the apostle was reproving," stated the magazine. "We believe to women, as well as to men, are granted gifts of the spirit and that these gifts should be exercised in public." Later articles defended the practice but clarified it. A woman could deliver a message in public but could not hold a church office, for that violated the "divine order," putting her between her husband and the world. Her husband was her "head." Such a transgression was "mannish." In the late 1930s the magazine reiterated that "prophecy was given to women . . . and this gift was on a higher plane than that of teaching," but "it is not theirs to rule over men."[54]

Likewise, John Roach Straton promoted Uldine Utley, a young female Bible teacher. Loyal to this "Joan of Arc of the modern religious world,"

Straton defended Utley as a "true prophetess," "one of the greatest Bible preachers." Straton responded to some southern religious leaders who were critical that Paul's prohibition of women preachers applied only to local circumstances and referred to unconverted women. The Bible, taken as a whole, he argued, was not against it.[55]

Billy Sunday employed women on his staff as Bible teachers and in organizational capacities. Once he chided someone for not placing women on the board of his 1921 Bluefield, West Virginia, campaign, because "their artistic ideas are superior to men's." Nell Sunday helped in her husband's evangelistic work for forty years, preaching when he was unable to, organizing committees, and taking care of the business side. She carried on a preaching ministry for twenty years after his death in 1935. The popular Winona Lake Bible Conference, associated with the Sundays, promoted the public ministry of women. Eva Ludgate, evangelist and Bible teacher, lectured there in 1924, and Grace Saxe in 1925 and 1931. Uldine Utley, converted under Aimee Semple McPherson in California and licensed as a Methodist preacher, spoke at Winona Lake in 1927. She also preached in Christian and Missionary Alliance, United Brethren, Methodist, Baptist, and Presbyterian churches. A favorite, Christabel Pankhurst, a British suffragist who had converted to premillennial fundamentalism and who began a public preaching ministry in 1921, spoke at Bible conferences, including Winona Lake, Moody Bible Institute, Straton's Calvary Baptist Church, and Mel Trotter's rescue mission. Her public ministry continued for twenty years. The number of women speakers at Bible conferences grew from about 27 in 1930 to about 50 in 1941.[56]

Even Bob Jones Sr., perhaps the most critical of the new woman, had a female evangelist on his staff. Mrs. Frances C. Allison spoke to both women's and men's groups, though "she never preaches but just talks," according to Jones. But in her "common sense talk" to men on a Sunday afternoon at the First Christian Church of Crawfordsville, Indiana, she took a text (David was the "sermon" topic) and afterward gave an invitation to accept Christ as savior. In 1929 at the Bob Jones College Bible Conference, the roster of speakers included two female Bible teachers. As late as 1936 Bob Jones Sr. believed that a "woman has her place in Christian work and has ample Christian liberty"; they could talk in prayer meeting, teach Sunday school, and take part in religious services, but they could not be pastors nor hold the "headship in religion." But he was not dogmatic; in reply to one inquiry on the subject he confessed he was not a Bible expert and suggested the person contact Moody Bible Institute.[57] His record on the role of women was far more ambiguous than his rhetoric.

One unusual ministry by a woman was Ida M. Hudson's advice column for young girls, which began in 1923 and lasted fifteen years in the *Sunday School Times*. Under the name "Mother Ruth," she dispensed advice to readers on a whole range of topics related to the home, family, and young people. The answers she gave the published letters revealed a very traditional evangelical outlook, but she did not avoid controversial topics. Born in Philadelphia, converted at eight, joining the Methodist Church at nine, Hudson led a life marred by tragedy and blessed with ministries that had worldwide impact. She served as a Sunday school superintendent, worked briefly in the business world, taught school, worked in a home for "fallen girls," served as president of the Philadelphia YWCA, spoke over the radio, and capped her ministry with writing for a major Christian periodical. Twice widowed, she never stopped her busy life. "With clear eyes she saw and understood the working of the enemy in the worldliness, Modernism, and downward tendencies of the day," one eulogist remarked. Her last public appearance was a speech to the Women's Auxiliary of the Philadelphia Fundamentalists.[58] Her life symbolized the contradictions within fundamentalism about the role of women; her message was traditional and welcomed, but her leadership in religion was a trend that conservative Protestants increasingly criticized in the interwar years.

Although marriage was important, fundamentalists valued full-time Christian service above it, and for some women that could mean being single. "Mother Ruth" wrote one young girl, fearful of remaining unmarried, that "God has had and has now a plan for your life." She challenged the girl: "Yes, it is a wonderful experience to be a wife and mother, and have a home; but have you ever considered the women who have been denied this experience, and the happiness they have had in allowing God to direct their way in life?" The home should have precedence over outside interests, another writer argued, unless a woman had to work because she was single. James M. Gray also honored the secular vocation of single Christian women, calling them a "shining star" during the Great Depression. Their salaries, he contended, kept thousands of homes solvent and aided churches financially as well. "She has been a helper of the poor, a supporter of missions, she has put a younger brother or sister through college, she has eased the burden of an aged parent, and she has been the beloved 'aunt' of scores of little ones," he exclaimed.[59]

Several factors help explain the openness of fundamentalists to women in various ministries. First, certain evangelical groups had been supportive of the idea—the Salvation Army, evangelical Quakers, United Brethren, and evangelists had worked with women in interdenominational Bible institutes and conferences. Cooperation with holiness and Pentecostal groups with traditions of female ministers encouraged it. As with differences over sacraments, church government, and theology, denominations disagreed about allowing women to preach, but they tolerated those differences. Fundamentalist urgency about evangelism often caused them to overlook gender concerns. Consequently, single women in full-time service were acceptable. Fundamentalist organizations were more open, less ecclesiastical, and could respond to opportunities as a popular religious movement. The innovation of the Bible schools, which helped laypeople, unintentionally gave women more opportunities. Also, the holiness and premillennial emphases placed a value on women's gifts such as prophesying, Joel's "prophesying daughters," part of the end times. In fact, opportunities for women in fundamentalism grew at a faster pace than in mainline churches between the wars because of the dynamic growth in fundamentalism during that period.[60]

The controversial ministry of Aimee Semple McPherson, a Pentecostal evangelist, pastor of Angelus Temple in Los Angeles, and founder of the International Church of the Foursquare Gospel, symbolized the ambiguity fundamentalists felt about women preachers. Some supported her; others despised her. With her dramatic preaching style, she represented, according to her biographer, an interplay of evangelicalism and popular culture. She conveyed a touch of "flapper" sex appeal, and "Vaudeville and Hollywood influenced her message and the ways she chose to deliver it." Commentators charged that her platform was a stage and the gospel "a Hollywood show"; her Sunday evening services had a vaudeville format. She had ministerial credentials from the Assemblies of God, Methodist, and Baptist licenses, and many Protestant denominations sponsored her evangelistic campaigns. Several key fundamentalists gave their blessing to her ministry: Paul Rader filled in for her, William Biederwolf spoke at Angelus Temple, Homer Rodeheaver performed there, and Billy Sunday dined at the parsonage. "She brought more souls into the kingdom," Bryan declared in 1924 about her previous year's ministry, "than were baptized at Pentecost." He, too, spoke at her church.[61]

Opposition to McPherson, by other fundamentalists, typified the hardening resistance to women in public ministry by the end of the 1930s. "Jesus Christ never intended for any woman to be put in the position of headship in religion," Bob Jones Sr. insisted, in a specific reference to McPherson. Arno Gaebelein called her "that snake in the grass." In addition, Bob Shuler and R. A. Torrey, fellow Los Angeles pastors, John Roach Straton, William Bell Riley, and organizations such as Moody Bible Institute, with its *Moody Monthly,* and BIOLA, with the *King's Business,* adamantly opposed her. Dispensationalists, such as the foregoing, argued that her practices of divine healing and "speaking in tongues" were not for this dispensation. Although fundamentalists shared her conservative theological beliefs, and McPherson was not a strict Pentecostal, other factors drove them apart: financial taint, her divorce, rumors of immoral behavior, association with Pentecostal emotionalism, and, finally, the fact that she was not just a woman, but a very popular one.[62]

In the fundamentalist uncertainty about women's role in the ministry, which vacillated between sanctioning and condemning women, the latter impulse of condemnation prevailed during the interwar period. The traditional view triumphed, but acceptance of separate spheres for men and women developed gradually. One scholar stated that "By World War II most Evangelicals could go a lifetime never having heard a woman preacher or pastor." She continued: "A female Bible Institute graduate who in 1910 may have pastored a small church or traveled as an itinerant revivalist would by 1940 more likely serve as director of religious education."[63]

Between the wars fundamentalists intensified their "female-subordination rhetoric," an emphasis on men as leaders, women as sinful, and wives as submissive. A 1933 article in *Moody Monthly* reflected a change from ambiguity and back to a clear Victorian view. The author argued that suffrage, equality, and birth control were part of a woman's effort "to cast off the yoke placed upon her by the 'blatant' curse," a reference to Eve's fall. "But the time has about come for controversy to cease as to 'women's rights.'" God intended women for "happy subordination" to men. "Equally important and interdependent are both men and women in their respective spheres. . . . Indeed nature has constituted and fitted each for so distinct and individual a service that transgression is ridiculous." He did concede, however, that the Old Testament judge of Israel, Deborah, was an exception. Eight years earlier Moody Bible Institute had excluded women from its pastors' course. Riley advised pastors to "suppress your wife's ambition, and quiet her tongue." After 1930, his Northwestern Schools taught against female ministers, although they still tolerated the practice. "God never called any woman to leave a husband, six or seven babies at home and run around over this country and preach the Gospel," Bob Jones Sr. thundered when he related an encounter he had with a woman in Atlanta, a wife and mother of seven who told him God had called her to be an evangelist.[64]

Several elements converged to bring about this dramatic reversal. Premillennial dispensationalism, which gave opportunities to women who had the gift of prophecy, also asserted that feminism was a danger. "The prominence of the female sex is shown to be foreshadowed in prophecy as a mark of the end of the age," James M. Gray editorialized in the *Moody Monthly*. Harry A. Ironside agreed. "Women craving what God in his infinite wisdom has forbidden them: authority, publicity, masculinity" indicated the end times. To that he added a special concern: "what a large place has the modern feminist movement secured in the affection of women who profess to believe the Bible." Consequently, confusion about gender did fuel their pessimism about society. For them, social conditions had to worsen in preparation for Christ's return. Their pessimism, however, did not keep them from trying to do something about it.[65]

In the late nineteenth and early twentieth centuries fundamentalists rhetorically called for a more muscular or masculine Christianity and attacked the feminine condition of the church. Revivalists were critical of this emphasis, although they did it often in a positive, not antifemale, manner. Evangelists often focused on men and what they considered men's special ability for religion. In churches most workers are women, Bob Jones Sr. observed, and men do not like "sissy" or "namby-pamby" organization. His revival campaigns, he believed, with his organized, business-like approach, yielded twice as many men converts as women.[66]

In the interwar period evangelism declined and with it public ministry opportunities for women. Fundamentalists concentrated instead on building institutions, less open to women, and on combating evolution and modernist theology. Debate with theological liberals intensified the literalist view of scriptures, which meant an exegesis less favorable to female ministers. In some measure women themselves acquiesced in the transition as social values changed and many favored domestic roles. The fundamentalist record on women for this time period compares favorably with that of mainline Protestantism, which was no more eager for women pastors than the conservatives. Moreover, American society in general, perhaps as a reaction to a rising feminism, favored subordination of women and separate spheres for men and women. Fundamentalists reflected what was happening to women in medicine, in higher education, and in the culture at large. Secular intellectuals and religious leaders, including modernists, expressed resentment about the influence of women on American culture.[67]

In a larger sense, mass culture, with its emphases on the pleasures of leisure and consumption, elevated the role of women outside the home, and fundamentalists, and others, reacted adversely to it. Working women, typically young, single, working-class women in the early twentieth century, had more social freedom and some money to indulge in entertainment. The percentage of women in the moviegoing audience, for example, increased from 40 percent in 1910 to 60 percent in 1920, and with the middle class increasingly attracted, it reached 83 percent by 1927, according to some estimates. Therefore, at some level, the attack on popular culture was part of the resistance to women's changing place in society.[68]

Likewise, the growing presence of women in the consumer society may have threatened fundamentalists. The consumer, most often pictured as female, had become a purchaser, rather than a producer of goods. Department stores represented, perhaps for some, freedom from home and a sense of rising expectations. As society became more feminized, this female consumption highlighted women's pleasure, disturbing to traditionalists such as conservative Christians. Desire and self-gratification had become commercialized, driven by erotic themes in advertising. Women were both objects and subjects of the consumer society. Their fulfillment was not ultimately possible because the need was not real, but imaginary, and therefore unattainable. According to Leigh E. Schmidt, "In the seasoned Protestant and republican rhetoric against luxury and consumption, women, in particular, were seen as especially vulnerable to fashion," and this feminization of consumption threatened men. Paradoxically, the consumer society that so many fundamentalists gladly embraced also elevated women in the culture to a degree they found disturbing.[69]

■

Popular culture proved to be a significant catalyst in shaping fundamentalist values between the wars. Secular amusements tainted young people, the home, women, cities, and colleges, and the consequences were nothing less than a crisis. Certainly fundamentalist criticism of "worldly" amusements is not news, but their ambiguous reaction to it is important to understand, for it clarifies their relationship to modernity and to American culture in general. An emphasis on personal holiness, an important tradition in fundamentalism, especially since the late nineteenth century, developed more strongly as urban culture confronted them with myriads of new, modern temptations. Tensions resulted as fundamentalists rejected the worldly forms of popular culture, but at the same time they were being changed by it. They tried to influence, control, and condemn popular culture, yet simultaneously they participated in it, imitated it, and competed with it. In the end, fundamentalism became a new, "modern" popular religious movement.

Within fundamentalism, tensions abounded as a consequence. They feared and attacked the city, where popular culture seemed most concentrated and threatening, yet urban America became the largest base for fundamentalist ministries. Colleges, corrupted by "worldliness" as well as by evolution and secularization, proved unsuitable, so conservative Christians founded their own with rules of conduct to protect students from popular vices. In some instances they adopted the secular form from mass culture, while rejecting the substance, and appropriated that form or technology for evangelism or other religious purposes. Theater, movies, and jazz, though roundly condemned, were adapted for fundamentalist use;

drama and film were evangelistic tools, and syncopation made gospel songs livelier and more appealing. Radio enjoyed a consensus of support; it seemed less morally ambiguous. Popular culture also forced fundamentalists to deal with gender issues. They fought feminism and spoke out against female roles in public ministries, but at the same time they still used women significantly, their public presence declining only gradually. Simultaneously they argued that women should be "elevated" by giving them a special place, in the home, relegating them to a separate sphere.

Fundamentalists' interaction with popular culture revealed critical traits of the popular religious force. They were not afraid to use modern techniques or technologies; they subtly appropriated aspects of therapeutic culture for their purposes. The question is what price, if any, did they pay? In fighting secularization and modernization did they transform themselves or synthesize into something essentially new? Historian R. Laurence Moore, examining the interplay of commercial culture and religion in the nineteenth century, concluded that "what was worldly and what was religious did several things at once, engaging in angry confrontation, somehow coexisting, commonly intermingling." Although neither religion nor the secular eclipsed the other, Moore continued, religion did unwittingly reduce itself to a position "on the cultural shelves as another commodity." Religion survived modernization and secularization through its innovations, but the result was a less redemptive force in American life.[70]

Some critics argue that conservative evangelicals, by attacking and condemning the world of entertainment, had little impact on secular society. By focusing on piety they neglected transforming popular culture; instead, they isolated it. Fundamentalists may have viewed entertainment as beyond redemption, but the biblical teaching, critics continue, is that all creation is sinful and redeemable. "Both abstinence and regulation restricted the transformative role of the church in culture," William Romanowski judged.[71]

Undeniably, the sheer power of popular amusements affected fundamentalists. By participating in the "cultural marketplace," they simplified their message, as Moody had before them, to appeal to the masses. Like journalism and photography, their gospel appeal was very adaptable to modern mass communications. Perhaps they oversimplified their message and relied too heavily on technology and methods and less on spiritual power. However, borrowing techniques did not mean for them borrowing ideas; fundamentalists never shared the modern worldview. Technology helped them spread their religious ideas without necessarily transforming the message. One scholar, Richard J. Mouw, has suggested that fundamentalists did not compromise with modernity but sought to bring to it a biblical perspective; they achieved not a secularity with a religious gloss but a "new religiosity with a secularist gloss." Adapting to aspects of therapeutic culture, fundamentalists, tapping their emotions more, softened the nature of their faith, he continued, and also showed a willingness to learn from modern knowledge.[72]

Fundamentalists' encounter with entertainment had other implications. Their denunciations of its corruption revealed a middle-class bias against both working-class values and the "sins" of the wealthy. One scholar has suggested that this critique of leisure activities functioned as a kind of church discipline, which did not operate effectively in a mass culture. A repudiation of popular culture, generally associated with the lower class, implicitly for some, elevated fundamentalists socially. Their reasons were moral, but for a few these reasons were also aesthetic. In another sense, fundamentalists strengthened a modern transformation of the meaning of class, one based less on material wealth and more on knowledge and communication; a modern "new class" emerged to rival traditional elites. Fundamentalists both mimicked and challenged the "new class" with their own "cultural resources"—technology, colleges, and periodicals.[73]

Fundamentalists' relationship to entertainment also raises the question of just how far these conservative evangelicals were from the mainstream. By adapting to facets of mass culture, they revealed much of their democratic or populist character; they enjoyed popular culture, or religious forms of it, as middle America did in the 1920s or 1930s. With mainline Protestants they shared a disgust for or an ambiguity about popular culture. Liberal Protestant Harry Emerson Fosdick attacked sexual promiscuity vigorously in the 1920s. According to biographer Robert Moats Miller, Fosdick had "Nice-Nelly standards" about the theater. Like some fundamentalists he was not prejudiced against drama, but also like some fundamentalists, such as Straton, he attacked the "rottenness" of the contemporary stage. As well, Fosdick shared a disgust with Hollywood's "sex-saturated" films and denounced jazz as "syncopated barbarity." Although a theological chasm separated fundamentalists and liberal Protestants, some cultural issues made them unwitting cobelligerents in social battles.[74]

Popular culture's influence also tended to distinguish fundamentalists from other Protestants. They were more enthusiastic about using new technologies than liberal Protestants, some of whom feared its effects. Concerns about vices evident in aspects of entertainment and amusements led fundamentalists to focus increasingly on personal morals, trying to protect Americans from a corrupt culture, while social gospelers emphasized social service as redemptive. Also, while fundamentalists tended to be more accommodating to middle-class and mass culture, Pentecostal and holiness groups resisted imitating them, instead nurturing their own views of piety and plain living.[75]

Curiously, the fundamentalist critique of popular culture found some common cause with secular elites. Around the beginning of the twentieth century, high and popular culture emerged as separate categories in American society, with class serving as a fault line. Cultural elitists—the wealthy, educated upper class—assailed popular culture, not for moral reasons as religious conservatives, but for the aesthetics. In the early twentieth century, however, some conservative intellectuals in the genteel tradition attacked theater, novels, and magazines as threats to morals and social order, as did fundamentalists. Their disdain derived from sources that were similar to those for fundamentalists: Christian asceticism in Western culture as well as anxieties about class and race. Later progressive critics of popular culture shared the moral and social concerns, but they added a humanitarian concern for the lower classes as victims of business and proposed that entertainment could be reformed. Many Christians shared that latter hope. Also, genteel and progressive critics, according to one scholar, "refused to accept different tastes in expressive arts from different social groups." They, as well as fundamentalists, sought to keep a single aesthetic standard—their own.[76]

Also in the interwar period, social scientists, as secular critics of mass entertainment, found common cause with fundamentalists. They, too, had a conflicting message about popular culture. It was an acceptable part of modern life, a typical product of urban America, but its improper use could lead to deviant behavior, juvenile delinquency, and adult problems. Like fundamentalists they worried about its impact on the young, the family, and the home and recognized the impact of the city. Moreover, those social scientists argued that deviance in popular culture came from within, not from outside forces. Fundamentalists, for a different reason, would agree, while progressive critics cited environmental causes. Even communist critics assailed jazz as debased, despite its connection to blacks, from whom they sought support.[77] As critics of popular culture, fundamentalists had a host of fellow warriors.

Conclusion

Fundamentalists responded with profound ambivalence to modernity. Despite their seeming losses in the 1920s, Nancy T. Ammerman has observed that for the future they "proved resilient and innovative. . . . They maintained a vibrant subculture in the midst of the modern world, a way of life both very modern and defiantly antimodern." In the theological, philosophical, and scientific realms they roundly denounced higher criticism and evolution, but in other cultural areas they were not so antagonistic. Rather, torn between the spiritual and the temporal, they resisted what they considered destructive threats and absorbed for their own purposes other features of the culture. This tension played out in a larger context as fundamentalists divided generally over their response to American culture. One group, strong premillennialists, condemned it, while others, such as Bryan, sought to guard it as the epitome of Christian civilization. These two groups, and those in between, did not follow a consistent course in their concern about modern American society. Their rhetoric masked contradictory behavior. Those who condemned it often imitated it, and those who sought to preserve it were selective about their perceived threats to it.[1]

As religious groups encounter modernity, three responses are possible—withdrawal, resistance, or accommodation. The Amish experience represents the first response, and conservative evangelicals the second; however, as James D. Hunter has argued, even with their resistance, "some yielding is likely." Such was the case for fundamentalists in the interwar period. In the end, their adjustments to mass culture did not alter the essentials of the Christian message, but it did have important consequences. Technology affected strategy; radio and film required a simpler message. Advertising and promotion of religion packaged it in less offensive ways. Public relations competed with the biblical notions of the "foolishness" of preaching (1 Cor. 1:18) and the reproach of Christ (Heb. 11:26).[2]

Adaptation to mass culture helped fundamentalists succeed; they latched on to democratic strategies, a key for American Christianity from the nineteenth century on. The controversial J. Frank Norris, for example, pastored two churches, one in Fort Worth, another in Detroit, and boasted it was the largest congregation ever under one leader, in 1946 a combined membership of 25,000. His use of radio and a newspaper, along with organizational skills, had brought results. After five years his Detroit church jumped from 800 to 6,193 members. He symbolized the fundamentalist growth for that era.[3]

The encounter with modern culture affected their values. Like liberal Protestants, they adapted to the business ethos of the 1920s and in doing so contributed to the process of economic modernization. Unwittingly, perhaps, they prized secular values such as efficiency, a mechanistic perspective that centered on results, and increasingly they lost sight of a purer spiritual vision. They needed the reminder that Paul had given believers in Corinthians: "For the weapons of our warfare are not carnal, but mighty through God" (2 Cor. 10:4). As a consequence, fundamentalists were less able to criticize the materialism of the postwar consumer society, unwilling or unable to confront some pernicious effects of advertising, and diminished in their capacity to challenge corporate America to behave as proper stewards of wealth. Though more resistant to secular popular culture and holding back what seemed to them as corrosive influences, fundamentalists nonetheless were subtly lulled into the leisure ethic and aspects of therapeutic culture. H. Richard Niebuhr's critique of fundamentalists serving a "Christ of culture" is only partially correct. Indeed, they sought to conserve old cultural ideas as biblical, but in the 1920s, in very modern fashion, they identified their faith, for better or worse, with new cultural ideas.[4]

In the end, fundamentalist reaction to modernity in the interwar period perhaps mirrored that of most Americans. Historian Lynn Dumenil has concluded that no simple generalizations describe sacred or secular reactions to the 1920s, for "Americans' response to change proved complex and ambivalent." Tensions and contradictions abounded within such varied groups as southern agrarians, the Lost Generation, modernists, and fundamentalists. Conservative evangelicals resisted elements of mass culture, as did secular critics of American society. They also often adapted to it, thereby desensitizing their estrangement toward the world and altering, albeit subtly, their practice of faith. Fundamentalists contributed to a process that diminished religion to a commodity for consumption or an experience to bring happiness. They became increasingly comfortable with modern therapeutic culture. As Marsden aptly observed: "Sometimes . . . to be Christian means to be at war with modernity; at other times it is the only key to living at peace with the American way of life."[5]

In the interwar years fundamentalists merely continued a tradition begun when George Whitefield, Charles G. Finney, and Dwight L. Moody linked religion, markets, and popular culture. Though their accommodation to modernity in the 1920s and 1930s may not have been that unbalanced, their legacy encouraged the post–World War II generation of evangelicals to push the cultural assimilation further. Toward the end of the century they focused less on Christ's Second Coming and holiness and more on politics and the family. Liberal arts higher education continued to be important. Evangelicals became more tolerant of cultural pluralism. They increasingly accepted the changing role of women, and after years of denouncing it as evil, they enlisted modern psychology, a touchstone of therapeutic culture, as an ally. One scholar concluded that by the 1970s secular culture had changed evangelicals more than evangelicals had changed secular culture. The momentum from consumption and leisure emphases between the wars eventually yielded a religious world inhabited by the electronic church, Christian theme parks, religious rallies in sports arenas to preserve marriage and family, and Christian psychologists touting over the radio their remedies for low self-esteem.[6]

Cultural historians debate the roles mass culture plays in American society. Radical critics decry the commodification and the homogenization of culture, often with a conspiratorial view toward "cultural entrepreneurs" who manipulate the masses. Other writers point to the benefits of mass culture: democratized leisure means more affordable pleasure and also consumers who could be not only passive "victims" but also active participants. Approval or disapproval of mass culture could often be traced to differing class perspectives: defending upper- or middle-class tastes or championing the working class. Michael Kammen concluded that "Conservatives were also inclined to view mass culture as mechanistic rather than organic (or natural), secular rather than spiritual, commercial rather than cerebral, vulgar rather than noble, appealing to the worst instincts in people rather than the best, ephemeral rather than enduring, and highly derivative rather than original." Given that view of secular mass culture, it is most ironic that religious conservatives appropriated mass culture for evangelism, their most noble calling.[7]

The moral and ethical dimensions of the consumer society have been shaped, according to Martin Marty, by three developments in Western society: the Bible, the Enlightenment, and the Industrial Revolution. Ideally, Hebrew prophets and the writers of the Gospels informed fundamentalists about consumerism, with teachings about community values (the body of believers), the importance of work, the use of material goods, and charity toward others. Prophets denounced excessive displays of wealth, and Christ commanded followers not to serve riches. Competing with these antimaterialistic values were ideas of the Enlightenment, which elevated individualism, freedom, and selfish desire. Adam Smith, for example, transformed self-interest into something positive. In the late nineteenth century, the Industrial Revolution, with its corporate competitiveness, born of social Darwinism, made it more difficult for Americans, and for fundamentalists as well, to maintain traditional cultural values.[8]

The moral dangers for fundamentalists in the interwar years in mixing religion and popular culture appear equally serious. Searching for pleasure originates with the self, as does the desire for material goods, and self-centeredness contradicts the Christian notion of love for others. Furthermore, if religion becomes a choice, like an amusement, it is reduced to a commodity. In the book of Ecclesiastes (2:1), the Preacher begins, "I said in mine heart, Go to now, I will prove thee with mirth, therefore enjoy pleasure: and behold, this also is vanity."[9]

Liberal theologian Harvey Cox has observed a "recurrent historical tension in evangelical Protestantism between storming the bastions of the secular world and leaving it to sink in its own sinfulness." Between the wars, fundamentalists—premillennial in eschatology, pessimistic about the world's course, and willing to abandon it—sought as outsiders to redeem individuals with the gospel. At the same time, as middle-class Americans, they delighted in the fruits of mass culture, when possible, for religious purposes. They tried to avoid worldliness but also sought respect from the world. "The result," according to Joel Carpenter, "has been a rather strange dance, so to speak, in which conservative evangelicals emulated many trends of popular culture while continuing to denounce America's transgressions." But he also concluded that fundamentalists "responded creatively to the trends in contemporary popular culture and made a lasting place for themselves in American Protestantism."[10] Their accommodation to mass culture reveals also what was most important to this religious group. They were willing to compromise certain traditions that defined the movement, such as premillennialism, holiness, and defense of the faith, but their flexibility with forms of consumption and pleasure strengthened their evangelistic emphasis, perhaps the movement's core. Fundamentalists adapted to the world, ironically, in order to save it.

In a larger historical context for fundamentalists, tensions between culture and religion existed as well as confusion about roles as either a mainstream or outsider religious group. Close identity with business and conservative politics made them part of dominant trends in America for much of the interwar period. In recent decades historians have concluded that politics were secondary to their theology and ideas. Nonetheless, their culture did affect their political views in the interwar years. They were pro-business in the prosperous 1920s and during the Great Depression. Traditional social reform had been abandoned; it was too identified with the social gospel. Fundamentalists decried the cultural erosion from modernism, evolution, and Bolshevism. At the same time they perceived the culture as corrupting, their patriotism abounded. They were determined to preserve American Christian civilization, and this post–World War I politicization had been built on nineteenth-century evangelical causes such as antislavery and temperance. Ironically, otherworldly premillennialists chose William Jennings Bryan, a politician, as their leader, which is further testimony that their behavior was governed by concern for culture.[11]

Political involvement in the 1920s centered on protecting American culture from various threats. Prohibition having been secured, fundamentalists fought to keep it. The anti-evolution campaign culminated in the

Scopes Trial in 1925, a technical legal victory, but a public relations disaster. Modernism and Bolshevism were also linked to evolution as antithetical to Christian civilization. In a decade when Congress severely restricted immigration, some fundamentalists were anti-immigrant. In the 1928 presidential campaign southern and northern fundamentalists joined the Hoover forces to keep Al Smith, Catholic and antiprohibition, out of the White House, although millions of conservative Protestants still voted for Smith for reasons of economics, geography, or class. In the 1930s, although a few fundamentalists expressed anti-Jewish views, most premillennialists were strongly pro-Zionist for prophetic, if not personal, reasons. As George Marsden concluded, "the political attitudes of most fundamentalists were much like those of their non-fundamentalist Republican neighbors." Historian Leo Ribuffo, historian of the old Christian right, also observed for the interwar era that "not all bigots were fundamentalists, and not all fundamentalists were bigots." If fundamentalists had not overcome the problem of race, neither had most proponents of the social gospel. Although their political views, at least for the 1920s, may have been more typical, their religious convictions drove them simultaneously to look heavenward for Christ to usher in the kingdom and for them to build a kingdom in America.[12]

In the depression decade fundamentalists could be both somber and sanguine in their political views. Some ministers viewed the economic woes as judgment for sin; as good premillennialists, they believed, and as current events confirmed to them, the world was getting worse. Speculation centered on Mussolini and Hitler as precursors of the Antichrist. In the minds of some fundamentalists, Roosevelt's New Deal, although credited for some economic recovery, also foreshadowed the end time, with its totalitarian bent and social engineering. The National Recovery Administration's blue eagle symbol could be, some argued, the "mark of the beast." But all was not lost. Fundamentalists believed spiritual revival was possible in the midst of misery; moreover, they believed Christ could return at any moment.[13]

In the end, their economic and political views were secondary to their faith, their conservative Protestant theology, and their defense of it.[14] To their credit, fundamentalists utilized mass culture to spread and defend what was most important to them. Christ, in the parable of the steward in

Luke's Gospel, praised an "unjust steward" for shrewd management of wealth: "for the children of this world are in their generation wiser than the children of light" (16:8). He then turned to his disciples and commanded them likewise to "make to yourselves friends of the mammon [riches] of unrighteousness" (16:9). In short, Christ wanted his disciples to imitate the good qualities found in this man of the world. Between the wars, as fundamentalists used secular techniques for spiritual purposes, they obeyed, albeit imperfectly, the spirit of that admonition.

Notes

Introduction

1. *New Republic* 60 (1929): 335, cited in Carter, "Fundamentalist Defense of the Faith," 205; Russell, *Voices of American Fundamentalism*, 47, 50.

2. Moore, *Selling God*, 9; Hunter, *American Evangelicalism*, 19.

3. Lears, *No Place of Grace*, xii–xiii, xv.

4. Clapp, "Why the Devil Takes Visa," 21, 23; Wuthnow, *God and Mammon in America*, 2–3.

5. Clapp, "Why the Devil Takes Visa," 22, 25; Campbell, *Romantic Ethic*, 1–2, 205–6, 217–19.

6. Campbell, *Romantic Ethic*, 223, 227.

7. Wuthnow, *God and Mammon in America*, 157–58, 160–61, 188–89; McDannell, *Material Christianity*, 6–8.

8. Hart, *Defending the Faith*, 6–8.

9. Carpenter, *Revive Us Again*, xii, 124–25; Hamilton, "Fundamentalist Harvard," 35, 37, 51, 261, 264; Larson, *Summer for the Gods*, 225–28.

10. Marsden, *Fundamentalism and American Culture*, 4, 6. For an excellent, expansive definition of fundamentalism see Brereton, *Training God's Army*, 165–70; Iannaccone, "Heirs to the Protestant Ethic?" 344; Carpenter, *Revive Us Again*, 16.

11. Carpenter, *Revive Us Again*, 6.

12. Ibid., 7–8.

13. Ibid., 5, 8.

14. Wenger, "Social Thought," 247–48, 286–93.

15. Carpenter, *Revive Us Again*, 9–10.

16. Still, "'Fighting Bob' Shuler," 619–20; Wenger, "Social Thought," 57, 73; Trollinger, *God's Empire,* 10.

17. Kammen, *American Culture,* xiii–xiv.

18. Marsden, *Fundamentalism and American Culture,* 184–95; Carpenter, *Revive Us Again,* 8, 33, 237.

Chapter One. Embracing the Consumer Society

1. Blanchard, *President Blanchard's Autobiography,* 182–85; Hulse, "Shaping of a Fundamentalist," 7.

2. Unidentified clipping, n.d., reel 4, Riley Papers.

3. Dixon, *Present Day Life,* 62–63; Marsden, *Fundamentalism and American Culture,* 118; Reynolds, *Walt Whitman's America,* 495.

4. William Bell Riley, "Sunday Night at the Sanctuary or the Picture Show?" *Baptist World* (Feb. 15, 1917), reel 2; clipping, *New Student,* April 13, 1927, reel 4; clipping, *Southern Methodist* (Nov. 27, 1929), reel 4, Riley Papers.

5. Massee, *Rekindling the Pentecostal Fire,* 80–81; Dr. W. E. Biederwolf, "Evangelism," *Bob Jones Magazine* 1 (June 1929): 3–4, 13, BJU Archives; William Evans, "Dr. Torrey As I Knew Him," *King's Business* 27 (Jan. 1936): 7, 15; clipping, *Miami Daily Metropolis,* 8 April 1922, Haymaker Papers.

6. *Sunday School Times* 65 (Feb. 10, 1923): 83–84; Dumenil, *Modern Temper,* 144.

7. Ad, *Moody Bible Institute Monthly* [hereinafter cited as *Moody Monthly*] 22 (Nov. 1921): 664; "Wise Hints from a Business Man," *Christian Workers Magazine* 20 (Jan. 1920): 377–88.

8. Editorials, *King's Business* 15 (Nov. 1924): 683–84, *King's Business* 17 (Dec. 1926): 701.

9. Editorials, *King's Business* 11 (Jan. 1920): 6–7, *King's Business* 13 (Jan. 1922): 3–4, Noll, *History of Christianity,* 382.

10. Smith, *Seeds of Secularization,* 128; Frank, *Less than Conquerors,* 129, 131–33.

11. Gilbert, *Perfect Cities,* 172, 174, 201, 206; Wauzzinski, *Between God and Gold,* 116.

12. Curtis, *Consuming Faith,* 254; Lundén, *Business and Religion,* 3, 35–36, 44–45, 51, 67–68, 83, 183.

13. Wauzzinski, *Between God and Gold,* 127, 219; Furniss, *Fundamentalist Controversy,* 27; see Wosh, *Spreading the Word.*

14. Editorial, *King's Business* 13 (July 1922): 649–50; Dorsett, *Billy Sunday,* 127–28; Chernow, *Titan,* 54, 56.

15. Wenger, "Social Thought," 257; Trollinger, *God's Empire*, 40, 88–89; clipping, *Crawfordsville (Ind.) Journal*, April 10, 1915, BJU Archives; Hankins, *God's Rascal*, 8; letters, John D. Rockefeller Jr. to J. Gresham Machen, March 7, 1922, Machen to Rockefeller, April 3, 1922, Machen to William A. Brown, April 3, 1924, Machen Papers; Moore, *Selling God*, 220.

16. T. C. Horton, "John Wanamaker—A Mastered Man," *King's Business* 18 (March 1927): 146–47; editorial, *Sunday School Times* 64 (Dec. 23, 1922): 797; "Editorial Notes," *Moody Monthly* 24 (Nov. 1923): 98; Clapp, "Why the Devil Takes Visa," 23; Schmidt, *Consumer Rites*, 162–63; Ershkowitz, *John Wanamaker*, 14, 30, 131.

17. Furniss, *Fundamentalist Controversy*, 57; clipping, *Grand Rapids (Mich.) Herald*, Sept. 12, 1940, Trotter Papers; unidentified clipping July 21, 1938, Syracuse, N.Y., reel 4, Rader Papers; Kenneth W. Russell II, "The Career of Mordecai F. Ham, Jr., 1900–1961," *Oklahoma Baptist Chronicle* (autumn 1982): 38, Charlotte Evangelistic Campaigns; Graham, *Just As I Am*, 34–35, 38.

18. Cochran, *Challenges to American Values*, 60; Lundén, *Business and Religion*, 57–58, 60; Hunter, *American Evangelicalism*, 6.

19. Gilbert, *Perfect Cities*, 201; clipping, *Montgomery (Ala.) Journal* [1921,] Scrapbook 6, BJU Archives; Massee, *Rekindling the Pentecostal Fire*, 65; editorial, *Standard*, March 27, 1915, 3, Biederwolf Papers.

20. W. E. Biederwolf, "The Organization of Local Committees," *Advance*, Jan. 27, 1916, 533–34, Biederwolf Papers; Biederwolf, "Raising Evangelistic Standards," *Expositor*, Oct. 1918, 32–33, Biederwolf Papers; letters, W. G. Haymaker to R. J. Charles, Nov. 27 and Dec. 22, 1928, Haymaker Papers.

21. Riley, *Crisis of the Church*, 17; Trollinger, *God's Empire*, 38, 156; Russell, *Voices of American Fundamentalism*, 79, 82, 103.

22. Lundén, *Business and Religion*, 58; Howard A. Banks, "Mixing Sound Doctrine and Modern Method," *Sunday School Times* 63 (Feb. 12, 1921): 88; editorial, "On Being Done with Bigness," *Sunday School Times* 63 (Aug. 6, 1921): 417–18.

23. Brereton, *Training God's Army*, 29, 32; William Bell Riley, "A Standardized Ministry," *Western Recorder*, July 3, 1941, reel 7, Riley Papers; Riley, *Menace of Modernism*, 156–59; editorial, "Crumbs from the King's Table," *King's Business* 20 (Dec. 1929): 567.

24. Unidentified clipping, Los Angeles, March 2, 1908, Trotter Papers; Jones, *"My Friends"*, 110; unidentified manuscript, "Regarding Mr. Rader," n.d., reel 4, Rader Papers.

25. Don Cochran, "Tabernacle Building," *Advance*, Jan. 27, 1916, 536–37, Biederwolf Papers; "Bringing Up Sunday School Efficiency," *Sunday School Times*

63 (Feb. 12, 1921): 89; "Efficiency Hints for Ministers," *Sunday School Times* 65 (March 31, 1923): 200.

26. Brereton, *Training God's Army,* 62; R. A. Torrey, "Training School for Evangelists and Personal Workers," *Advance,* Jan. 27, 1916, 535, Biederwolf Papers.

27. Straton, *Gardens of Life,* 204–5; editorial, *Sunday School Times* 68 (April 24, 1926): 245–46; J. Gresham Machen, "Christianity and Liberty: A Challenge to the 'Modern Mind,'" *Forum and Century* 85 (March 1931): 163–64, Machen Papers.

28. Perrett, *America in the Twenties,* 348–55; Hunter, *American Evangelicalism,* 24, 37.

29. Brereton, *Training God's Army,* 152; Marsden, "Evangelicals, History and Modernity," 98; Frank, *Less than Conquerors,* 132, 212–13.

30. Cochran, *Challenges to American Values,* 60; Fox and Lears, introduction, xi–xii; Curtis, *Consuming Faith,* xiii, 11–12, 14, 254, 276, 278.

31. Stout, *Divine Dramatist,* xvii–xviii, xxii; Gilbert, *Perfect Cities,* 172, 187, 189, 192, 199, 201, 206; see Lambert, *"Pedlar in Divinity."*

32. Clipping, *Gloversville and Johnstown (N.Y.) Morning Herald,* April 28, 1916, Scrapbook 4, BJU Archives; William Bell Riley, "Sunday Night at the Sanctuary or the Picture Show?" *Baptist World,* Feb. 15, 1917, reel 2, Riley Papers.

33. Lundén, *Business and Religion,* 67–68; editorial, *Wheaton Record,* Oct. 6, 1926; address, J. Gresham Machen, "Westminster Theological Seminary: Its Purpose and Plan," Sept. 25, 1929, Machen Papers.

34. Brereton, *Training God's Army,* vii–ix.

35. "Editorial Notes," *Moody Monthly* 23 (July 1923): 508.

36. Mother Ruth, "Girls' Problems of Today," *Sunday School Times* 65 (Aug. 25, 1923): 495–96; Emily H. Butterfield, "'Selling' the New Testament to Young Women," *Sunday School Times* 66 (Feb. 9, 1924): 86.

37. Perrett, *America in the Twenties,* 350–52; Pease, *Responsibilities of American Advertising,* vii, 8, 21, 41–42, 170; Lears, "From Salvation," 6–9, 16–17, 22–23, 28.

38. Clapp, "Why the Devil Takes Visa," 22–23, 25–26.

39. Ibid., 23.

40. Lundén, *Business and Religion,* 76, 78, 83; Brereton, *Training God's Army,* 23–25.

41. Gilbert, *Perfect Cities,* 187; Lundén, *Business and Religion,* 39; Hankins, "Saving America," 34–35; M. B. Williams, "Advertising an Evangelistic Cam-

paign," *Advance,* Jan. 27, 1916, 536; William Edward Biederwolf, "The Organization of Local Committees," *Advance,* Jan. 27, 1916, 533–34, Biederwolf Papers.

42. Letter, William Jennings Bryan to George W. Moore, May 13, 1925, Bryan Papers; "A New York Broker" and "The Gospel in the 'Ad' Column," *Sunday School Times* 64 (Jan. 14, 1922): 20; Jones, *"My Friends",* 89; unidentified clipping, n.d., Scrapbook 6, BJU Archives; Allen Taff, "What Bob Jones College Has Meant to Me," *Bob Jones Magazine* 3 (Jan. 1931): 6–7, BJU Archives; Pease, *Responsibilities of American Advertising,* 52.

43. J. Richard Olson, "The Pulpit and the Press," *Moody Monthly* 23 (Jan. 1923): 204–5; "Editorial Notes," *Moody Monthly* 31 (Dec. 1930): 169–70.

44. Joseph A. Richards, "Jesus Christ—The Great Advertisement," *King's Business* 15 (March 1924): 139–40; Richards, "Spirituality in Church Advertising," *Moody Monthly* 28 (Jan. 1928): 225–26.

45. Frank, *Less than Conquerors,* 215–17, 219; Lears, "From Salvation," 17, 22–23, 28; Buswell, *Lamb of God,* 75; G. V. Kirk, "Report to the Board of Trustees," June 14, 1932, Buswell Papers.

46. Pease, *Responsibilities of American Advertising,* 88, 108–11, 148, 151.

47. Furniss, *Fundamentalist Controversy,* 41–42; Straton, *Fighting the Devil,* v–vi, viii; report of the Biederwolf Evangelistic Campaign, "The Plainfield Way," 1916, Biederwolf Papers; Harold C. Chase, "Conducting Children's Meetings," *Advance,* Jan. 27, 1916, 541–42, Biederwolf Papers; "A Working Program," *Expositor,* Oct. 1918, 19–21, Biederwolf Papers; and letter, Homer Rodeheaver to Billy Sunday, Oct. 20, 1929, Sunday Papers; Russell, *Voices of American Fundamentalism,* 118–19, 127.

48. Grace Bryan Hargraves, unpublished Bryan biography, 4, Bryan Papers.

49. Article, Paul Rader, *National Radio Christian Announcer,* May 1926; unidentified clipping, Syracuse, N.Y., July 21, 1938, reel 2, Rader Papers.

50. *World-Wide Christian Courier,* Dec. 1929, reel 3, Rader Papers; "Los Angeles Opens Arms to Paul Rader," *National Radio Christian Announcer,* Jan. 1926, reel 2, Rader Papers.

51. Joseph B. Bowles, "A National Conference on Church Publicity," *Moody Monthly* 23 (Jan. 1923): 206–7; Furniss, *Fundamentalist Controversy,* 41; *Pentecostal Herald,* July 7, 1915, 12–13, Biederwolf Papers; D. M. Shreve, "The Biederwolves of Christianity," *Worth While,* Jan. 1918, 285–87, 321–23, Biederwolf Papers.

52. Biederwolf, "Raising Evangelistic Standards," *Expositor,* Oct. 1918, 32–33, Biederwolf Papers; "Baptists Lowering Their Colors," *Watchman-Examiner,*

Dec. 6, 1928, reel 5, Riley Papers; Turner, "Fundamentalism," 148–49; Jones, *"My Friends"*, 22–23.

53. "The College Point Development[:] Site of Bob Jones College," *Birmingham (Ala.) News,* May 6, 1926, Scrapbook 8, BJU Archives; "An Epoch in Education: Facts about the Bob Jones College," [1928?,] BJU Archives; Perrett, *America in the Twenties,* 360; Tommy Smith, interview by Dan Turner, May 17, 1988, in possession of Turner; Gilbert, *Perfect Cities,* 192–93, 195–96, 198.

54. Letters, Bob Jones [to friends], Feb. 26, 1926, Dec. 7, 1926, *Bob Jones Magazine* 1 (Feb. 1929), BJU Archives; Smith, interview, May 17, 1988; Dalhouse, *Island in the Lake,* 38–39.

55. Brereton, *Training God's Army,* 154; Beale, *In Pursuit of Purity,* 233–35; Furniss, *Fundamentalist Controversy,* 126; Still, "'Fighting Bob' Shuler," 157; William Bell Riley, "The Bookmakers, Part II," *Pilot,* Sept. 1940, reel 6, Riley Papers; inside front cover, *Bob Jones Magazine* 1 (June 1928), BJU Archives.

56. "Editorial Notes," *Christian Workers Magazine* 20 (July 1920): 851–52; editorial, *King's Business* 14 (Oct. 1923): 3; Quiggle, "Moody Magazine," 342–47; Eskridge, "Campus Life," 78–87.

57. Miller, *Harry Emerson Fosdick,* 379; Marty, *Irony of It All,* 210, 215–16, 290; Gilbert, *Perfect Cities,* 207; Wuthnow, *Struggle for America's Soul,* 61–62; Carpenter, "Shelter in the Time," 67; Russell, *Voices of American Fundamentalism,* 53.

58. Editorial, *King's Business* 14 (Sept. 1923): 901; "The Christian and Radio," *Moody Monthly* 31 (Nov. 1930): 161; "Editorial Notes," *Moody Monthly* 38 (Oct. 1937): 55.

59. "An Unique Institution," n.d., BJU Archives; William Jennings Bryan, "The Radio," n.d., Bryan Papers; address, Bryan, "All," March 12, 1922, Bryan Papers; "Editorial Notes," *Moody Monthly* 34 (Sept. 1933): 3; "Notes on Open Letters," *Sunday School Times* 65 (14 April 1923): 230, 235.

60. Floyd B. Johnson, "The National Radio Chapel: What It Is," *National Radio Chapel Announcer,* Dec. 1925; "Radio Schedule over WHT," *World-Wide Christian Courier,* June 1926 and Feb. 1929, reel 2; Clarence Jones, "Paul Rader: Pioneer of Gospel Broadcasting," manuscript and *World-Wide Christian Courier,* April 1930, reel 3, all Rader Papers.

61. Franklin C. E. Lundquist, "Bridging Space by Radio," and editorial, "This Is a New Day," *National Radio Chapel Announcer,* Dec. 1925; Floyd B. Johnson, article in special Easter issue, *National Radio Chapel Announcer,* 1926; Paul Rader, "What about a Radio Church?" *World-Wide Christian Courier,* July 1926

and Feb. 1929, reel 2; see also Clarence Jones, "Paul Rader: Pioneer of Gospel Broadcasting," manuscript, reel 3, all Rader Papers.

62. Kenneth Lloyd Williams, "Broadcasting the Gospel from Los Angeles," *Sunday School Times* 65 (April 14, 1923): 231; Torrey, *God of the Bible,* viii.

63. Ralph E. Stewart, "The Romance of the Radio," *Moody Monthly* 39 (May 1939): 492.

64. Still, "'Fighting Bob' Shuler," 248–51; "An Unique Institution" and inside front cover, *Bob Jones Magazine* 2 (June 1930), BJU Archives; *Indianapolis Star,* April 20, 1996; pamphlet, Stewart P. MacLennan, "Universal Air-Mindedness," n.d., reel 5, Riley Papers.

65. Watt, *Transforming Faith,* 35; Brereton, *Training God's Army,* xvi, xviii, 82, 84, 154; *Wheaton College Record,* Sept. 21, 1922, and Jan. 30, 1927; letter, Charles A. Blanchard to Charles E. Gremmels, Sept. 13, 1922, Blanchard Papers; inside back cover, *Bob Jones Magazine* 1 (Nov. 1928), BJU Archives; Bob Jones Jr., interview by Dan Turner, Jan. 26, 1987, and May 28, 1987, in possession of Turner; "Evangelistic Club Hand Book," Association of Business Men's Evangelistic Clubs, 1921–1929, Patterson Papers.

Chapter Two. Reflecting on the Consumer Society

1. Allen, *Only Yesterday,* 144; Susman, *Culture As History,* 129–31; Barton, *Man Nobody Knows,* preface, 143.

2. Barton, *Man Nobody Knows,* 8–9, 68, 75, 104, 108, 111, 140.

3. Ibid., 59–60, 86, 126.

4. Letters, Charles Scribner's Sons official [unintelligible] to Bruce Barton, April 8, 1924, Barton to Mary Converse, Jan. 19, 1924, to Herbert S. Baker, Oct. 3, 1925, to D. L. Chambers, Jan. 16, 1926, to Louis Ludlow, Aug. 10, 1938, *New York Times Book Review,* May 10, 1925, Barton Papers.

5. Allen, *Only Yesterday,* 148; Susman, *Culture As History,* 129; Wauzzinski, *Between God and Gold,* 150, 156; Marty, *Noise of Conflict,* 443–46; Lundén, *Business and Religion,* 95; Lears, "From Salvation," 32, 36; Hofstadter, *Anti-intellectualism in American Life,* 116.

6. *New York Times Book Review,* May 10, 1925, Barton Papers; Lundén, *Business and Religion,* 126, 153; Lears, "From Salvation," 29–30; Marty, *Noise of Conflict,* 46.

7. *New York Times Book Review,* May 10, 1925, Barton Papers; Lears, "From Salvation," 30–31, 36.

8. Lears, *No Place of Grace,* 304; Parrish, *Anxious Decades,* 78–80; Lears, "From Salvation," 29–34, 37; Lundén, *Business and Religion,* 102–3.

9. Susman, *Culture As History,* 128; sermon by Rader, "Who Put the Ad in Advertising?" n.d., reel 4, Rader Papers; *Christian Herald* illustration, Jan. 1, 1927, reprinted in Lundén, *Business and Religion,* 10; letter, Paul Maynard to Bruce Barton, Nov. 15, 1926, Barton Papers.

10. Rev. Robert Clark, "The God That Nobody Knows," *Moody Monthly* 30 (March 1930): 335–36; letters, Hewitt H. Howland to Bruce Barton, Jan. 18, 1924, Edward W. Grilley Jr. to Barton, July 30, 1926, Charles W. Koller to Barton, Sept. 3, 1927, Barton Papers; "Notes on Open Letters," *Sunday School Times* 69 (Feb. 12, 1927): 86.

11. Iannaccone, "Heirs to the Protestant Ethic?" 344–45, 351, 360–61; Schmidt, *Consumer Rites,* 188, 191.

12. Letters, William Jennings Bryan to William C. Bobbs, April 22 and 29, 1925, Bryan Papers; Gaebelein, *Christ We Know,* 3–4; Rev. Fred J. Mitchell, "The Man *I Know,*" *Moody Monthly* 27 (Dec. 1926): 165–66; "Notes on Open Letters," *Sunday School Times* 69 (June 11, 1927): 358.

13. Amos H. Gottschall, "The Book Entitled: 'The Man Nobody Knows' under the Dissecting Knife," self-published, n.d., 1, 6, 7, 12–13, Barton Papers.

14. Letters, Gertrude [no last name given] to Bruce Barton, Jan. 30, 1925, Bartholomew Timlin OJM to Barton, Feb. 10, 1925, Heath Sale to *Woman's Home Companion,* Aug. 21, 1925, Barton Papers; unidentified clipping, n.d., Barton Papers; Marty, *Noise of Conflict,* 52–55; Miller, *American Protestantism,* 26, 34–35.

15. Dixon, *Present Day Life,* 49, 59; Trollinger, *God's Empire,* 65; Riley, *Messages for the Metropolis,* 25, 170, 219; Riley, *Crisis of the Church,* 121; Gray, *Great Epochs of Sacred History,* 115, 122–23; unidentified clipping, [1914?,] Bob Jones Sr. sermon, Scrapbook 1, BJU Archives.

16. Wenger, "Social Thought," 260–63, 280; Rader, "Panics Impossible? A Dangerous Idea?" *National Radio Chapel Announcer,* Jan. 1926, reel 2, Rader Papers; "President L. R. Akers of Asbury College Addresses the Students at Bob Jones College November 2, 1929," *Bob Jones Magazine* 2 (Dec. 1929): 2, 15–16, BJU Archives.

17. Wenger, "Social Thought," 261–63; Straton, *Menace of Immorality,* 88–89; Massee, *Gospel in the Ten Commandments,* 19–20, 86–88, 119, 122–23; unidentified clipping, April 23, 1926, reel 4, Riley Papers.

18. Clipping, *Andalusia (Ala.) Star,* Feb. 25, 1927, Bob Jones Sr., "Perils of America," lecture-sermon, Scrapbook 6, BJU Archives; Straton, *Gardens of Life,*

75–76, 114; Straton, *Menace of Immorality*, 207, 211; Torrey, *Gospel for Today*, 182.

19. Torrey, *Gospel for Today*, 182–83; Straton, *Menace of Immorality*, 207; Wenger, "Social Thought," 261–62.

20. Wenger, "Social Thought," 261; Massee, *Gospel in the Ten Commandments*, 64–65, 119; "President L. R. Akers of Asbury College Addresses the Students at Bob Jones College," 2, 15–16, BJU Archives; "Notes on Open Letters," *Sunday School Times* 71 (Dec. 21, 1929): 738.

21. "Letters from a Farm Mother to Her Son at College," *Sunday School Times* 70 (May 12, 1928): 296.

22. Clipping, H. L. Mencken, 1926, Barton Papers; "Notes on Open Letters," *Sunday School Times* 65 (April 14, 1923): 230; Mother Ruth, "Girls' Problems of Today," *Sunday School Times* 65 (May 5, 1923): 283.

23. Furniss, *Fundamentalist Controversy*, 178; questionnaire, Ivan J. Fahs to Mrs. Sidney Butz, Dec. 1, 1982, Charlotte Evangelistic Campaigns; "Special Tabernacle Bulletin," [1937,] reel 4, Rader Papers; Still, " 'Fighting Bob' Shuler," 157–58, 400.

24. Editorial, *Bob Jones Magazine* 3 (Jan. 1931): 1, BJU Archives; Turner, "Fundamentalism," 124n; Bob Jones Jr., interview, 26 Jan. 1987 and 28 May 1987.

25. Report by Bob Jones Sr. to the Board of Trustees, Jan. 9, 1933, BJU Archives; letters, Bob Jones Sr. to Howard Bailey, March 20, 1933, Bob Jones Jr. to J. Willett Vess, Nov. 5, 1982, BJU Archives; Turner, "Fundamentalism," 124, 129; Dalhouse, *Island in the Lake*, 45–47.

26. Watt, *Transforming Faith*, 50–54; Riley, *Philosophies of Father Coughlin*, 1, 17, 19, 21–22, 24, 27, 53; Ironside, *Miscellaneous Papers*, 48, 50–52; "Editor's Page," *Bob Jones Magazine* 2 (April 1930): 1, BJU Archives; clippings, *Dothan (Ala.) Eagle*, Jan. 4, 1932, and unidentified clipping, [1932?,] Scrapbook 9, BJU Archives; Jones, *Things I Have Learned*, 67–68.

27. "Editorial Notes," *Moody Monthly* 31 (Oct. 1930): 52, *Moody Monthly* 31 (April 1931): 390, *Moody Monthly* 34 (May 1934): 396; Paul W. Rood, "Around the King's Table," *King's Business* 27 (June 1936): 211; "Notes on Open Letters," *Sunday School Times* 73 (Aug. 22, 1931): 458.

28. Riley, *Philosophies of Father Coughlin*, 38, 53; clipping, "Technocracy in the Church," [1930s,] reel 5, Riley Papers; clipping, Karl Morgan Block, "Broadcasting the Seed," *Southern Churchman*, May 22, 1937, reel 6, Riley Papers; editorial, *Courier*, Jan. 28, 1933, reel 1, Rader Papers.

29. Editorial, *Courier*, Jan. 28, 1933, reel 1, Rader Papers; "Editorial Com-

ment," *King's Business* 21 (Aug. 1930): 373, and *King's Business* 21 (Dec. 1930): 553; "Editorial Notes," *Moody Monthly* 32 (Dec. 1931): 160.

30. Clipping, *Associate Reformed Presbyterian* [1932,] reel 4, Riley Papers; "Notes on Open Letters," *Sunday School Times* 74 (May 21, 1932): 274; "Bruce Barton's Imaginary Heroes," *Sunday School Times* 74 (July 30, 1932): 397–98; "Overdoing the 'Nobody Knows,'" *Sunday School Times* 77 (Aug. 24, 1935): 545–46.

31. Editorial, "Our Economic Life in Light of Christian Ideals," *Moody Monthly* 33 (July 1933): 481–82; Rev. F. W. Haberer, "Socialism and First Century Christianity," *Moody Monthly* 33 (July 1933): 482–83; William F. E. Hitt, "Why the Hard Times?" *Moody Monthly* 33 (Nov. 1932): 105–6; Carter, "Fundamentalist Defense of the Faith," 193.

32. Paul W. Rood, "Around the King's Table," *King's Business* 26 (Nov. 1935): 403; "Editorial Notes," *Moody Monthly* 31 (April 1931): 390–91, and *Moody Monthly* 35 (July 1935): 506; H. E. Eavey, "The Business Man: His Place in Business and in the Kingdom of God," *Moody Monthly* 38 (May 1938): 463–64.

33. Carpenter, "Shelter in the Time," 65, 68; James O. Buswell, "What Will the Larger Wheaton Mean?" *Bulletin of Wheaton College,* Oct. 1936, 3–10; editorial, *Wheaton Record,* May 28, 1930; Hamilton, "Fundamentalist Harvard," 32.

34. Brereton, *Training God's Army,* 84; letter, Will H. Houghton to Mrs. William M. Sunday, Nov. 12, 1935, Sunday Papers; clipping, William Bell Riley, "A Standardized Ministry," *Western Recorder,* July 3, 1941, reel 7, Riley Papers; Trollinger, *God's Empire,* 88, 92, 98; Riley, *Problems of Youth,* 5.

35. Donald M. Taylor and Mildred M. Cook, "The Gospel in Industry," *King's Business* 27 (Nov. 1936): 416–17; W. G. Haymaker, "Big Business and the Real Gospel," *Christian Workers,* Jan. 1937, 1–4, Patterson Papers; Dick LeTourneau, "When Toccoa Was Thinking of God," *Moody Monthly* 40 (Oct. 1939): 64–65.

36. Longfield, *Presbyterian Controversy,* 217; clipping, *Charlotte News,* Feb. 24, 1932, Patterson Papers; pamphlet, "Gospel Fellowship Association," [late 1930s?,] BJU Archives.

37. Letter, Bob Jones Sr. to "Dear Friend," April 18, 1933, BJU Archives; clipping, *Chattanooga Times,* Aug. 22, 1939, Scrapbook 9, BJU Archives; pamphlet, Jones, "Persecuted for Orthodoxy" [1940,] BJU Archives; Turner, "Fundamentalism," 133–34, 137–38, 140; Dalhouse, *Island in the Lake,* 47–49.

38. Turner, "Fundamentalism," 136; letters, John Sephus Mack to Bob Jones Sr., Oct. 20, 1936, Nov. 9, 1936, and Sept. 7, 1938, BJU Archives.

39. Letters, Bob Jones Sr. to John Sephus Mack, Oct. 23, 1936, Nov. 20, 1936,

and Sept. 9, 1938; Bob Jones Sr., quoted in *Time*, Feb. 22, 1937, 38, 40, BJU Archives.

40. Riley, *Pastoral Problems*, 32–33, 46, 48–51; clipping, *Charlotte Observer*, Nov. 11 and 16, 1934, Ham Papers; Vernon Patterson, interview by Ivan J. Fahs, Jan. 3, 1983, and Grady Wilson, interview by Fahs, Jan. 3, 1983, Ham Papers.

41. "1940 Periodical" ads, large postcard ad for Bob Jones College [c. 1940,] inside front cover, *King's Business* 30 (June 1939), BJU Archives; "Notes on Open Letters," *Sunday School Times* 73 (Dec. 19, 1931): 714.

42. Carpenter, "Shelter in the Time," 67; pamphlet, Jones, "Persecuted for Orthodoxy," [1940,] BJU Archives; Furniss, *Fundamentalist Controversy*, 126; Carl F. H. Henry, "The Clergy and the 'Word Business,'" *Moody Monthly* 39 (Jan. 1939): 258.

43. Carpenter, "Shelter in the Time," 70–71; Ralph E. Stewart, "The Romance of the Radio," *Moody Monthly* 39 (May 1939): 492–93, 503; "Editorial Notes," *Moody Monthly* 40 (Oct. 1939): 60; "Notes on Open Leters," *Sunday School Times* 74 (Jan. 23, 1932): 42; clipping, *Kingsport (Tenn.) Times*, Aug. 6, 1933, Scrapbook 9, BJU Archives; Turner, "Fundamentalism," 151; editorial, *Wheaton Record*, Dec. 5, 1939; memo, James Oliver Buswell to fieldmen, Nov. 14, 1939, Buswell Papers.

44. Letters, W. E. Burchard to J. Frank Norris, Feb. 16, 1931, Norris to J. Gresham Machen, May 30, 1933, Norris Papers; clipping, [*Baptist and Commoner*, 1932,] Norris Papers; Hankins, *God's Rascal*, 8, 90–91.

45. Carpenter, "Shelter in the Time," 71; Charles G. Trumbull, "The Miracle Gospel Broadcast of America," *Sunday School Times* 80 (Oct. 22, 1938): 747; Goff, "'We Have Heard,'" 69–71.

46. Carpenter, *Revive Us Again*, 130–31.

47. Marsden, "Evangelicals, History, and Modernity," 98; Marty, *Noise of Conflict*, 174; Marty, *Irony of It All*, 194, 215; Hunter, *American Evangelicalism*, 6, 11; Wuthnow, *Struggle for America's Soul*, 61–62.

48. Wauzzinski, *Between God and Gold*, 221–22.

49. Schmidt, *Consumer Rites*, 14, 297.

50. Lundén, *Business and Religion*, 44; Fox and Lears, introduction, xii; Lears, "From Salvation," 6–9, 22–23; tract, [1925?,] by "A Witness," "The Dangerous Glamor of Prosperity: What It Does to Believers," Scrapbook 46, reel 4, Riley Papers; Jones, *Comments on Here*, 99–100.

51. Unidentified clipping, n.d., reel 3, Rader Papers; Carpenter, *Revive Us Again*, 140.

52. Miller, *American Protestantism*, 22; Lundén, *Business and Religion*, 33,

35–36, 51, 179–80; see Curtis, *Consuming Faith;* Marty, *Noise of Conflict,* 52–55, 318.

53. Carwardine, "'Antinomians' and 'Arminians,'" 282–307.

54. Moore, *Selling God,* 10, 236.

Chapter Three. Encountering Popular Culture

1. "If a Minister Loves 'the World'?" *Sunday School Times* 62 (July 10, 1920): 377.

2. Wagner, *Adversaries of Dance,* 5, 27, 32, 47, 79, 84, 115–17, 141, 199, 236–37, 276, 321, 392.

3. Carpenter, *Revive Us Again,* 57–64.

4. See Moore, *Selling God,* 5–6, for a discussion of the meanings of culture; Kammen, *American Culture,* 17–18, 21–22, 24–25, 50–51, 53–54, 70–71, 73, 76–77.

5. Coben, *Rebellion against Victorianism,* 3–4; Miller, *Harry Emerson Fosdick,* 418; Ownby, *Subduing Satan,* 122; Jones, *"My Friends,"* 118; Allan A. Zaun, "Wheaton in a Modern World," *Wheaton Alumni News,* May–June 1937, 1–2; Carpenter, *Revive Us Again,* 58.

6. Straton, *Menace of Immorality,* 12; Buswell, "A Christian College," *Bulletin of Wheaton College,* Nov. 1926, Buswell Papers; Jones, *Things I Have Learned,* 150; Will H. Houghton, "Youth's Page," *Moody Monthly* 36 (Sept. 1935): 21.

7. Longfield, *Presbyterian Controversy,* 118–19, 122; editorial, *King's Business* 16 (March 1925): 104; Louis T. Talbot, "Around the King's Table," *King's Business* 25 (Jan. 1934): 3; "Editorial Notes," *Moody Monthly* 37 (Feb. 1937): 287–88, 38 (Nov. 1937): 111; Rev. Harold L. Lundquist, "The Decline of the American Home," *Moody Monthly* 38 (Nov. 1937): 115, 123.

8. Straton, *Menace of Immorality,* 191; Straton, *Fighting the Devil,* 5–9; Machen, "Skyscrapers and Cathedrals," *McCalls* 59 (Oct. 1931): 23, 118, Machen Papers; Ammerman, "North American Protestant Fundamentalism," 17; Romanowski, *Pop Culture Wars,* 24.

9. Blanchard, *President Blanchard's Autobiography,* 180–81; Paul Rader, "Christ or Crime," *National Radio Chapel Announcer,* Dec. 1925, reel 2, Rader Papers; unidentified clipping, [1907,] reel 2, Riley Papers.

10. Ownby, *Subduing Satan,* 167–69, 193; Jones, *Perils of America,* 7–11.

11. Straton, *Gardens of Life,* 113–14; Riley, *Revival Sermons,* 151, 156; Riley, *Pastoral Problems,* 28–29.

12. John Bunyan Smith, "Christ in the Cities," *King's Business* 26 (July 1935):

245; Paul W. Rood, "Around the King's Table," *King's Business* 27 (March 1936): 82; Straton, *Gardens of Life,* 208–09.

13. Unidentified clipping, [1922,] Scrapbook 7, BJU Archives; "The College Point Development[:] Site of Bob Jones College," promotional brochure, BJU Archives.

14. Blanchard, *President Blanchard's Autobiography,* 59; C. A. Blanchard, "Summaries of Religious Attitudes of Colleges," 1919, Blanchard Papers.

15. James O. Buswell, "A Plea for Puritanism," n.d., Buswell Papers; Buswell, "The Discipline Problem," *Wheaton Alumni Quarterly,* Dec. 1933, 9–12; editorials, Oct. 2, 1929, and Jan. 29, 1930, *Wheaton Record;* Helen Torrey Renich, interview by Robert Shuster, May 17, 1982, Graham Center Archives.

16. "An Epoch in Education: Facts about the Bob Jones College," [1928?,] form letter, office manual, [1944?]; Bob Jones, "A Frank Word about Our Boys and Girls," *Bob Jones Magazine* 1 (April 1929): 1, 23; A. H. Perpetuo, "The Uniqueness of Bob Jones College," *Bob Jones Magazine* 3 (Jan. 1931): 14–15; *Bob Jones College Catalogue, 1934–1935,* 13; clipping, anonymous [Dorothy Seay], "Accent on Sin," *American Mercury,* Sept. 1940, 16–23, all BJU Archives.

17. Massee, *Rekindling the Pentecostal Fire,* 53; Massee, *Evangelistic Sermons,* 74; Miller, *American Protestantism,* 18.

18. Clippings, *Methodist,* [1930,] reel 5, Riley Papers; Rev. R. Banes Anderson, "Why People Do Not Go to Church," *Presbyterian,* Feb. 17, 1938, reel 6, Riley Papers; Ironside, *Miscellaneous Papers,* 20–21; Torrey, *Gospel for Today,* 77–78.

19. "Editorial Notes," *Moody Monthly* 30 (Oct. 1929): 58; Straton, *Menace of Immorality,* 162–65, 167–68.

20. Miller, *American Protestantism,* 18; Buswell, *Lamb of God,* 86–87; Carpenter, *Revive Us Again,* 60.

21. Massee, *Sunday Night Talks,* 53; Prof. F. E. West, "Why I Do Not Smoke," *Bob Jones Magazine* 2 (Jan. 1930): 14, 16, BJU Archives; clipping, July 1, 1929, *Methodist,* reel 5, Riley Papers.

22. Dixon, *Present Day Life,* 84–85, 117, 119–22; letters, James Oliver Buswell to Howell Evans, June 7, 1926, to Esther M. Hart, May 16, 1928, Buswell Papers; Straton, *Menace of Immorality,* 119–25, 128–29.

23. Dixon, *Present Day Life,* 107–8; Straton, *Fighting the Devil,* 30; Straton, *Menace of Immorality,* 31; clipping, *St. Petersburg (Fla.) Times,* [Oct.–Nov. 1922?,] Scrapbook 7, BJU Archives; Jones, *Two Sermons to Men,* 8–10; unidentified clipping, n.d., reel 5, Riley Papers; "Editorial Notes," *Moody Monthly* 35 (May 1935): 410; Dumenil, *Modern Temper,* 135; Gorman, *Left Intellectuals,* 92.

24. Moore, *Selling God,* 6; Marty, *Noise of Conflict,* 174–75.

25. Ownby, *Subduing Satan,* 143–44, 163; Moore, *Selling God,* 149–50, 152; Trumbull, *Victory in Christ,* 108–9.

26. Unidentified clipping, n.d., reel 1, Riley Papers; Dixon, *Present Day Life,* 87–88; Rausch, *Arno C. Gaebelein,* 205–6, 212, 222; "Editorial Notes," *Moody Monthly* 34 (June 1934): 444.

27. Curtis, *Consuming Faith,* 237–38; unidentified clipping, 1934, Ham Papers; Straton, *Fighting the Devil,* 136, 143, 146, 159, 164.

28. Straton, *Fighting the Devil,* 171–73; Richard J. Kraft, "Foundations of Football at Wheaton," in "Centennial Notebook," [1960,] 3–4, 7, Wheaton College Archives; editorial, *Wheaton College Record,* Nov. 26, 1924; William J. Jones, "Speaking of Athletics," *Wheaton Alumni Quarterly,* Oct. 1930, 6; unidentified clipping, n.d., reel 1, Riley Papers.

29. Carpenter, *Revive Us Again,* 22.

30. Ibid., 23; see Sidwell, "History of the Winona Lake Bible Conference."

31. Unidentified clippings, n.d., reels 1 and 4, Riley Papers; Straton, *Fighting the Devil,* 226; Dan Gilbert, "Pitfalls for Faith in Modern Magazines," *Sunday School Times* 79 (July 24, 1937): 523.

32. Dixon, *Present Day Life,* 126–28; editorial, *Sunday School Times* 64 (Jan. 7, 1922): 1–2.

33. Clipping, William Bell Riley, "The Bookmakers," Part II, *Pilot,* Sept. 1940, reel 6, Riley Papers; ad for Paul Rader novel, "Big Bug," reel 4, Rader Papers; Carpenter, "Shelter in the Time," 66–67; Philip E. Howard, "Fleming H. Revell, Publisher," *Sunday School Times* 73 (Nov. 7, 1931): 620; Romanowski, *Pop Culture Wars,* 38; Carpenter, *Revive Us Again,* 24–25.

34. See Stout, *Divine Dramatist;* Dorsett, *Billy Sunday,* 147.

35. Romanowski, *Pop Culture Wars,* 41–43.

36. Massee, *Gospel in the Ten Commandments,* 133–34; clipping, *Waterloo Daily Courier,* [1909?,] reel 3, Riley Papers; unidentified clipping, Oct. 1907, reel 2, Riley Papers; *Good News,* Sept. 29, 1917, reprint from *Christian Standard,* reel 1, Rader Papers; Gray, *Prophecy and the Lord's Return,* 35–36; Straton, *Fighting the Devil,* 64–65, 70, 72, 101–6, 108.

37. Straton, *Fighting the Devil,* 64–65, 70, 72, 101–6, 108.

38. Clipping, *Literary Digest,* Feb. 20, 1909, reel 2, Riley Papers; unidentified clipping, n.d., reel 1, Riley Papers.

39. A Former Actor, "From a Christian Home to the Stage," *Sunday School Times* 69 (April 9, 1927): 231; "An Emotional Pagan Goes in for Experience," *Sunday School Times* 69 (April 16, 1927): 247.

40. Straton, *Fighting the Devil,* 81, 238; Straton, *Menace of Immorality,* 33;

Riley, *Crisis of the Church,* 169; H. Harold Kent, "The Young Christian and Worldly Amusements," *Moody Monthly* 22 (Oct. 1921): 613; Sivert Ness, "Dramatic Plays in the Christian Church—A Timely Warning by a Correspondent," *Moody Monthly* 32 (Jan. 1932): 245; J. A. Morris Kimber, "Shall He Go in for College Dramatics?" *Sunday School Times* 62 (July 17, 1920): 397.

41. Rausch, *Arno C. Gaebelein,* 205; Bob Jones Jr., interview, Jan. 26, 1987, and May 28, 1987; Turner, "Fundamentalism," 209, 211.

42. Bob Jones III, interview by Dan Turner, June 3, 1987, in possession of Turner; Karl Keefer, interview by Dan Turner, July 27, 1987, in possession of Turner; pamphlet, Bob Jones Sr., "Why . . . Bob Jones University Was Founded," [1949,] BJU Archives; chapel sermon, Bob Jones Sr., Nov. 18, 1948, manuscript, copy in possession of Dan Turner; Bob Jones Jr., interview, Jan. 26, 1987, and May 28, 1987; Turner, "Fundamentalism," 215, 217–18.

43. Jones [Jr.], *Cornbread and Caviar,* 47–48; Turner, "Fundamentalism," 122, 153–54, 283–84, 288, 303, 314; *Bob Jones College Catalogue, 1934–1935,* 13, BJU Archives; clipping, *Chattanooga Times,* May 28, 1939, in scrapbook "Publicity, 1929–1939," BJU Archives.

44. Turner, "Fundamentalism," 223, 226, 229n, 273, 367; Katherine Stenholm, interview by Dan Turner, June 8, 1987, in possession of Turner; Jones, *Cornbread and Caviar,* 37–38, 68.

45. Turner, "Fundamentalism," 137, 226, 228, 367; clipping, Donald E. Hoke, "The Unusual Dr. Bob," *Christian Life,* Feb. 1953, 24–27, 92–93, BJU Archives.

46. Turner, "Fundamentalism," 137, 292; Jones, *Cornbread and Caviar,* 44, 46; Bob Jones Jr., interview, Jan. 26, 1987, and May 28, 1987; Elizabeth Edwards, interview by Dan Turner, May 28, 1987, in possession of Turner; Keefer, interview, July 27, 1987.

47. Turner, "Fundamentalism," 233–34, 261, 265; booklet, *The Classic Players* (Cleveland, Tenn.: Bob Jones College, 1939), BJU Archives; unidentified clipping, n.d., in scrapbook "Publicity, 1929–1939," BJU Archives.

48. Turner, "Fundamentalism," 221, 252, 373–74.

49. Lawrence Levine quoted in Romanowski, *Pop Culture Wars,* 89, 92, 95–96.

50. Turner, "Fundamentalism," 307, 309, 311; Bob Jones III, interview, June 3, 1987.

51. Bob Jones III, interview, June 3, 1987; Jones, *Cornbread and Caviar,* 47–48; Turner, "Fundamentalism," 144n, 353n, 355, 360–61; Keefer, interview, July 27, 1987.

52. Turner, "Fundamentalism," 213–14, 351n, 352; Bob Jones III, interview, June 3, 1987; Jones, *Cornbread and Caviar,* 47–48.

53. Jones, *Cornbread and Caviar,* 57.

54. Turner, "Fundamentalism," 354; Buswell, *Lamb of God,* 75; Bob Jones Sr., chapel message, May 13, 1949, copy in possession of Dan Turner.

55. Letter, Bob Jones Sr. to Bernie Stanton, July 3, 1940, BJU Archives; chapel message, Bob Jones Sr., May 13, 1949.

56. *Wheaton Record,* April 27, 1927, editorials, Jan. 11, 1928, June 6, 1928, April 29, 1931, April 4, 1939.

57. Stenholm, interview, June 8, 1987.

Chapter Four. Judging Popular Culture

1. Stenholm, interview, June 8, 1987; unidentified clippings, n.d., reels 1 and 7, Riley Papers; Hart, *Defending the Faith,* 164; Graham, *Just As I Am,* 9–10.

2. Moore, *Selling God,* 221–22; Romanowski, *Pop Culture Wars,* 50–51, 130.

3. Romanowski, *Pop Culture Wars,* 116, 118, 136–37.

4. Moore, *Selling God,* pp. 222–23.

5. Ibid., 224; Perrett, *America in the Twenties,* 227; Romanowski, *Pop Culture Wars,* pp. 138–39.

6. MacLean, *Behind the Mask,* 111; Lears, *No Place of Grace,* 27–28; Romanowski, *Pop Culture Wars,* 143–44.

7. Haskell is arguing from a feminist perspective. Interestingly, fundamentalists today, as in the interwar period, sometimes are cobelligerents with secular voices against certain aspects of modernity. See Haskell, "Movies and the Selling," 126–33.

8. Unidentified clipping, n.d., reel 5, Riley Papers; William H. Short, "The Social Influence of Motion Pictures," *Moody Monthly* 35 (Sept. 1934), 12; Riley, *Wives of the Bible,* 76; *Good News,* Dec. 29, 1917, reel 1, Rader Papers; Shuler, *What New Doctrine,* 170; "Semi-weekly Broadcaster," Oct. 28, 1937; letter, James Oliver Buswell to Mrs. F. C. Card, Jan. 29, 1927, Buswell Papers.

9. "Editorial Notes," *Christian Workers Magazine* 20 (May 1920): 696–97; L. Ray Miller, "May Christians Attend Picture Shows?" *Moody Monthly* 25 (March 1925), 317–18; Rev. William Evans, "Hollywood's Scale of Values," *Moody Monthly* 38 (Nov. 1937): 120.

10. "Review and Comment," *King's Business* 20 (April 1929): 166; "Editorial Notes," *Moody Monthly* 38 (Nov. 1937): 111; Edward L. Jeambey, "Are the Movies Really a Menace?" *Moody Monthly* 27 (July 1927): 535–36; clipping, [*Bel-*

lingham (Wash.) American, Nov. 1927,] Scrapbook 8, BJU Archives; Moore, *Selling God,* 224–25; Perrett, *America in the Twenties,* 228.

11. Moore, *Selling God,* 225; Perrett, *America in the Twenties,* 224–26.

12. Perrett, *America in the Twenties,* 226–27; Moore, *Selling God,* 226–30.

13. Letter, William Jennings Bryan to Will Hays, March 7, 1923, Bryan Papers; Shuler, *Bob Shuler Met These,* 144–45; Still, " 'Fighting Bob' Shuler," 156; clipping, *American Baptist,* April 13, 1927, reel 4, Riley Papers; unidentified clipping, [1934,] Ham Papers.

14. " 'Cleansing' the Movies," *Sunday School Times* 65 (Jan. 13, 1923): 17; editorial, *King's Business* 13 (Oct. 1922): 989–90; editorial, *King's Business* 15 (April 1924): 196–97; "Around the King's Table," *King's Business* 25 (Oct. 1934): 339; unidentified clipping, [1925,] reel 4, Riley Papers; Riley, *Problems of Youth,* pp. 14–15.

15. Torrey, *Gospel for Today,* 6–7; "Editorial Notes," *Moody Monthly* 21 (Dec. 1920): 150–51; editorial, *King's Business* 15 (April 1924): 196–97.

16. "Notes on Open Letters," *Sunday School Times* 62 (May 8, 1920): 258, 62 (May 15, 1920): 274, 62 (May 22, 1920): 286, 62 (May 29, 1920): 298, and 70 (March 24, 1928): 186.

17. Moore, *Selling God,* 160–61; Lundén, *Business and Religion,* 74; letters, Charles M. Sheldon to William Jennings Bryan, Dec. 29, 1922, Bryan to Austin W. Smith, Feb. 5, 1923, Bryan Papers; Romanowski, *Pop Culture Wars,* 133.

18. Videotape of three 16mm silent films, Rader Papers; film, "That Blessed Hope," 1943, produced by Visualized Scripture Institute, Riley Papers; letters, J. J. McCarthy to Mrs. W. A. Sunday, March 7, 1924, H. Rodeheaver to Billy Sunday, December 7, 1931, Sunday Papers; *Wheaton Record,* Dec. 9, 1938; memo, James Oliver Buswell to field men, Nov. 14, 1939, Buswell Papers; inside back cover, *Bob Jones Magazine* 1 (Nov. 1928), BJU Archives.

19. Bob Jones [Sr.], *Two Sermons to Men,* p. 59; Turner, "Fundamentalism," 341–42; Jones [Sr.], *Unbeatable Game,* 18; clippings, *Philadelphia Courier,* May 2 and 12, 1925, *Philadelphia North American,* May 10, 1925, *Philadelphia Daily News,* May 12, 1925, Scrapbook 8, BJU Archives.

20. Clippings, *Philadelphia Courier,* May 12, 1925, *Philadelphia Daily News,* May 12, 1925, unidentified, May 1925, *Philadelphia Evening Ledger,* May 1925, Scrapbook 8, BJU Archives; Bob Jones Sr., chapel message, Nov. 18, 1948. In 1950 BJU started a cinema department, and its director, Katherine Stenholm, trained at Stanley Kramer's film lot in Hollywood and at the University of Southern California film school. See Turner, "Fundamentalism," 342–43, 347–48.

21. Romanowski, *Pop Culture Wars,* 111, 124, 139; Horowitz, "Alliance of Convenience," 554.

22. Mother Ruth, "Girls' Problems of Today," *Sunday School Times* 70 (Jan. 28, 1928): 49; "Editorial Notes," *Moody Monthly* 25 (Dec. 1924): 148; Moore, *Selling God,* 231–32.

23. Moore, *Selling God,* 231–34.

24. Ibid., 231–32; "The *Sunday School Times* Radio Directory," *Sunday School Times* 73 (May 30, 1931): 313; "Notes on Open Letters," *Sunday School Times* 74 (Jan. 23, 1932): 42; "Editorial Notes," *Moody Monthly* 34 (Sept. 1933): 3.

25. Rev. O. L. Markman, "Religious Lessons of the Radio," *Moody Monthly* 25 (Sept. 1924): 10–11, Ralph E. Stewart, "The Romance of the Radio," *Moody Monthly* 39 (May 1939): 492; "Editorial Notes," *Moody Monthly* 27 (Feb. 1927): 276.

26. Mother Ruth, "Girls' Problems of Today," *Sunday School Times* 70 (Jan. 28, 1928): 49; Perrett, *America in the Twenties,* 232; Tindall, *America,* 1035.

27. C. Louise Woodbridge, "Why Is Jazz Degrading?" *Sunday School Times* 70 (Sept. 29, 1928): 562; Turner, "Fundamentalism," 118–19; "Rules of the Bob Jones College," [1931,] BJU Archives.

28. Robert Harkness, "The Chaos of Modern Music," *Sunday School Times* 68 (Sept. 25, 1926): 552; Massee, *Sunday Night Talks,* 79–80; Trumbull, *Prophecy's Light on Today,* 120.

29. "Editorial Notes," *Moody Monthly* 33 (March 1933): 299–300; "Rules of Bob Jones College," Scrapbook 1933–1937, BJU Archives; editorial, *Wheaton Record,* Dec. 5, 1939.

30. Richard Oliver, "Youth and Music," *World-Wide Christian Courier,* June 1928, reel 2, Rader Papers.

31. "Editorial Notes," *Moody Monthly* 24 (Oct. 1923): 49; editorial, *King's Business* 11 (Aug. 1920): 734.

32. Herbert G. Tovey, "Modern Gospel Songs," *King's Business* 13 (Dec. 1922): 1241–43.

33. Dumenil, *Modern Temper,* 144; sermon, William Edward Biederwolf, March 3, 1929, reel 4, Rader Papers; Rev. D. W. Askew, "The American Home— Save It!" *Bob Jones Magazine* 2 (Sept. 1929): 5–6, 8, BJU Archives; Rev. Harold L. Lundquist, "The Decline of the American Home," *Moody Monthly* 38 (Nov. 1937): 115; pamphlet, Charles A. Blanchard, "Christianity in the Home," (Bible Institute Colportage Association, n.d.), Blanchard Papers; DeBerg, *Ungodly Women,* 103, 148.

34. Ownby, *Subduing Satan,* 103–4; DeBerg, *Ungodly Women,* 62, 97.

35. Unidentified clipping, 1934, Ham Papers; Dixon, *Present Day Life,* 65; Jones, *Perils of America,* 24; Straton, *Menace of Immorality,* 106, 117; letter by W. L. Peters, "Preservation of American Womanhood," *Moody Monthly* 31 (Jan. 1931): 253; Rev. Harold L. Lundquist, "The Decline of the American Home," *Moody Monthly* 38 (Nov. 1937): 115.

36. Tindall, *America,* 1035; Straton, *Menace of Immorality,* 46; "Editorial Notes," *Moody Monthly* 38 (July 1938): 560; DeBerg, *Ungodly Women,* 117, 148.

37. Dumenil, *Modern Temper,* 137–81; Perrett, *America in the Twenties,* 157; J. F. Collins, "Notes and Comments," *Bob Jones Magazine* 2 (Sept. 1929): 3, 13–15, BJU Archives; letter by W. L. Peters, "Preservation of American Womanhood," *Moody Monthly* 31 (Jan. 1931): 253; Miller, *Harry Emerson Fosdick,* 425; Tindall, *America,* 1035.

38. Unidentified clipping, New York, 1916, Scrapbook 2, BJU Archives; unidentified clipping, Waterloo, Iowa, March 1926, BJU Archives; clipping, *Birmingham (Ala.) News,* May 6, 1926, Scrapbook 8, BJU Archives; "Editor's Page," *Bob Jones Magazine* 1 (July 1929): 1, 2 (Jan. 1930): 1, BJU Archives; Straton, *Menace of Immorality,* 45, 49–50; Riley, *Problems of Youth,* 23; "Editorial Notes," *Moody Monthly* 34 (July 1934): 491–92.

39. Rev. Albert Kinzler, "What about Hair-Bobbing?" *Moody Monthly* 24 (Aug. 1924): 605, editorial, 25 (Nov. 1924): 101; editorial, *Wheaton College Record,* Jan. 18, 1924.

40. Tindall, *America,* 1036–40; Perrett, *America in the Twenties,* 158.

41. DeBerg, *Ungodly Women,* 51; *Wheaton College Record,* Feb. 10, March 25, and April 25, 1920; unidentified clipping, New York, 1916, Scrapbook 2, BJU Archives.

42. "Editorial Notes," *Moody Monthly* 35 (Sept. 1934): 3–4; Trumbull, *Prophecy's Light on Today,* 122–23; Straton, *Menace of Immorality,* 173; J. Floyd Collins, "What Price Lawlessness," *Bob Jones Magazine* 1 (June 1929): 5–6, 10–13, BJU Archives; clipping, *Evansville (Ind.) Courier,* Oct. 10, 1920, Trotter Papers; Watt, *Transforming Faith,* 96.

43. Parrish, *Anxious Decades,* 155–56; Perrett, *America in the Twenties,* 159.

44. Parrish, *Anxious Decades,* 155; Perrett, *America in the Twenties,* 160, 164; Riley, *Problems of Youth,* 67, 73; Buswell, *Lamb of God,* 76n; "Editorial Notes," *Moody Monthly* 31 (March 1931): 336.

45. "Editorial Notes," *Christian Workers Magazine* 20 (Jan. 1920): 360; Massee, *Gospel in the Ten Commandments,* 105–6; clipping, *Montgomery (Ala.) Advertiser,* June 3, 1921, Scrapbook 6, BJU Archives.

46. Florence Nye Whitwell, "A Modern College Question—and the Answer," *Sunday School Times* 77 (June 1, 1935): 372–73; Edward L. Jeambey, "Why Companionate Marriage Will Not Work," *Moody Monthly* 28 (Oct. 1927): 58–59.

47. DeBerg, *Ungodly Women,* 117; unidentified clipping, [1911?,] Scrapbook 1, BJU Archives; Mother Ruth, "Girls' Problems of Today," *Sunday School Times* 66 (Oct. 25, 1924): 636–37; 67 (June 20, 1925): 404; 76 (Dec. 22, 1934): 836–37; 76 (Dec. 13, 1934): 820–21.

48. Unidentified clipping, March 11, 1910, reel 2, Riley Papers; Riley, *Youth's Victory,* 58; Straton, *Menace of Immorality,* 78–79.

49. DeBerg, *Ungodly Women,* 148; Miller, *Harry Emerson Fosdick,* 420–21; Perrett, *America in the Twenties,* 157; J. Floyd Collins, "Notes and Comments," *Bob Jones Magazine* 2 (June 1930): 4–5, BJU Archives; editorial, *Wheaton College Record,* Feb. 18, 1925; Bessie Morris Johnson, "The Business Girl As I See Her," *National Radio Chapel Announcer,* Jan. 1926, reel 2, Rader Papers.

50. Perrett, *America in the Twenties,* 154, 156; Straton, *Gardens of Life,* 37; Straton, *Menace of Immorality,* 94–95.

51. Unidentified clipping, n.d., reel 2, Riley Papers; Riley, *Wives of the Bible,* vii–viii; Mother Ruth, "Girls' Problems of Today," *Sunday School Times* 69 (June 11, 1927): 364; Jones, *Perils of America,* 10; DeBerg, *Ungodly Women,* 97.

52. Hamilton, "Women, Public Ministry," 179, 188.

53. Massee, *Rekindling the Pentecostal Fire,* 108–10; clipping, *Literary Digest,* May 13, 1926, reel 4, Riley Papers; Riley, *Pastoral Problems,* 165–67; Trollinger, *God's Empire,* 102–5, 107, 110.

54. Grant Stroh, "Practical and Perplexing Questions," *Moody Monthly* 27 (Jan. 1927), 247; Rev. Graham Gilmer, "Should Christian Women Speak or Lead in Prayer in Our Churches?" *Moody Monthly* 28 (Jan. 1928): 223–24; J. W. Newton, "Women's Work in the Gospel," *Moody Monthly* 37 (Sept. 1936): 19–20.

55. Russell, *Voices of American Fundamentalism,* 49, 53, 233n.

56. Letterhead for "Sunday Evangelistic Campaign Norfolk and Portsmouth, Virginia," Jan. and Feb. 1920, Billy Sunday to [Mrs. Sunday], [May–June, 1921,] note in support of Mrs. Sunday's "permit" [to preach?], Nov. 2, 1935, Sunday Papers; Hamilton, "Women, Public Ministry," 176; Hassey, *No Time for Silence,* 126, 130–31, 136; program brochure, "Thirteenth Annual Conference," Brotherhood of Rescue Mission Superintendents, Jan. 2–19, 1921, Trotter Papers.

57. Clipping, *Crawfordsville (Ind.) Journal,* April 12, 1915, Scrapbook 2, "Bible Conference Speakers"; *Bob Jones Magazine* 1 (April 1929): 4; letter, Bob Jones Sr. to J. W. Stabler, May 30, 1936, all BJU Archives.

58. "Mother Ruth Called Home," *Sunday School Times* 81 (Feb. 11, 1939): 89; Laura Z. LeFever, "The Secret of Mother Ruth's Answers to Girls' Problems," *Sunday School Times* 81 (April 22, 1939): 271–72.

59. Hamilton, "Women, Public Ministry," 174; Mother Ruth, "Girls' Problems of Today," *Sunday School Times* 74 (Sept. 3, 1932): 466; *Wheaton College Record,* Feb. 10, 1920; "Editorial Notes," *Moody Monthly* 34 (Sept. 1933): 4.

60. Hamilton, "Women, Public Ministry," 175–78, 180–82, 187–88; Hassey, *No Time for Silence,* 125–29; Brereton, *Training God's Army,* 99, 129–31.

61. Blumhofer, *Aimee Semple McPherson,* 6, 16–18; address, William Jennings Bryan, Southern Bible Conference, Miami, Feb. 17, 1924, Bryan Papers.

62. Clipping, *Waterloo (Iowa) Evening Courier,* Nov. 17, 1926, Scrapbook 8, BJU Archives; letter, A. C. Gaebelein to A. C. Dixon, Jan. 20, 1925, Dixon Papers; editorial, *Moody Monthly* 22 (Nov. 1921): 648; Blumhofer, *Aimee Semple McPherson,* 163, 221, 223–24; Still, "'Fighting Bob' Shuler," 204–6, 209–11.

63. Hamilton, "Women, Public Ministry," 179; Marsden, "Evangelicals, History and Modernity," 127; Hassey, *No Time for Silence,* 138, 140; Green, "From Sainthood to Submission," 539–56.

64. E. Myers Knoth, "Woman's Rebellion and Its Consequences," *Moody Monthly* 34 (Oct. 1933): 55; Hamilton, "Women, Public Ministry," 172, 179; Hassey, *No Time for Silence,* 142; Riley, *Pastoral Problems,* 110–11; Trollinger, *God's Empire,* 105–6; Bob Jones Sr., "Sermon on the Home," n.d., BJU Archives.

65. "Editorial Notes," *Moody Monthly* 31 (June 1931): 486; Ironside, *Miscellaneous Papers,* 21–22; DeBerg, *Ungodly Women,* 122, 125, 127.

66. DeBerg, *Ungodly Women,* 86, 97; Bendroth, *Fundamentalism and Gender,* 3, 5–6, 13–14, 32; clipping, *Montgomery (Ala.) Journal,* [1921,] Scrapbook 6, BJU Archives.

67. Hassey, *No Time for Silence,* 137–39, 143; Bendroth, *Fundamentalism and Gender,* 32; Hamilton, "Women, Public Ministry," 180–86; Marsden, "Evangelicals, History and Modernity," 127; Dumenil, *Modern Temper,* 199; see DeBerg, *Ungodly Women.*

68. Romanowski, *Pop Culture Wars,* 67–69.

69. Felski, *Gender of Modernity,* 61–90; Schmidt, *Consumer Rites,* 10.

70. Marty, *Irony of It All,* 215; Mouw, *Consulting the Faithful,* 63; Moore, *Selling God,* 10, 268.

71. Romanowski, *Pop Culture Wars,* 44, 48.

72. Gilbert, *Perfect Cities,* 207; Mouw, *Consulting the Faithful,* 63–64, 66, 74; Dumenil, *Modern Temper,* 195.

73. Ownby, "Mass Culture, Upper-Class Culture," 126; Wuthnow, *Struggle for America's Soul*, 61–62.

74. Miller, *Harry Emerson Fosdick*, 419, 422, 425, 436–40.

75. Marty, *Irony of It All*, 290–91; Marty, *Noise of Conflict*, 174–75; Watt, *Transforming Faith*, 138.

76. Gorman, *Left Intellectuals*, 13, 15, 37, 41, 46–47, 51; Romanowski, *Pop Culture Wars*, 19–20.

77. Gorman, *Left Intellectuals*, 84–90, 96, 106–7, 133.

Conclusion

1. See Marsden, *Fundamentalism and American Culture*, 124–38; Ammerman, "Dynamics of Christian Fundamentalism," 14.

2. Hunter, *American Evangelicalism*, 16–17.

3. Hankins, *God's Rascal*, 7–8, 91.

4. Wauzzinski, *Between God and Gold*, 221–22; Niebuhr, *Christ and Culture*, 102; for a more detailed discussion of religion, consumer culture, and popular culture see Oberdeck, *Evangelist and the Impresario*.

5. Dumenil, *Modern Temper*, 198; Lears, *No Place of Grace*, xvi; Marsden, "Evangelicals, History and Modernity," 95.

6. Hunter, *American Evangelicalism*, 130, 132; Watt, *Transforming Faith*, 4, 13, 138.

7. Kammen, *American Culture*, 47, 62, 72, 84, 90–91, 164, 177; Ownby, *American Dreams in Mississippi*, 1–2, 5–6, 161.

8. Rosenblatt, introduction, 6–7; Schor, "What's Wrong with Consumer Society?" 37; Marty, "Equipoise," 178–81.

9. "Lovers of Pleasure," sermon to faculty and staff, Bob Jones III, Sept. 10, 1999, notes in possession of author.

10. Cox, "Warring Visions," 65; Carpenter, "Shelter in the Time," 75; Carpenter, *Revive Us Again*, xii–xiii, 242.

11. Marsden, *Fundamentalism and American Culture*, 206–8.

12. Ibid., 208–11; Ribuffo, *Old Christian Right*, 87, 249; Harvey, *Redeeming the South*, 206.

13. Carpenter, *Revive Us Again*, 90, 93–94, 101, 106, 110, 118.

14. Carter, "Fundamentalist Defense of the Faith," 212; Wenger, "Social Thought," 286.

Bibliography

Manuscripts

Billy Graham Center Archives, Wheaton College, Wheaton, Illinois
    William Edward Biederwolf Papers
    Charlotte Evangelistic Campaigns Research Project Records, 1915–1983
    Mordecia F. Ham Papers, microfilm copy
    Willis G. Haymaker Papers
    Vernon William Patterson Papers
    Daniel Paul Rader Papers, microfilm copy
    William Bell Riley Papers, microfilm copy
    Reuben A. Torrey Papers
    Mel Trotter Papers

Bob Jones University Archives, Mack Library, Bob Jones University, Greenville, South Carolina
    Collections of newspaper clippings, printed matter, correspondence, and miscellaneous materials
    William and Helen Sunday Papers, microfilm copy

Manuscripts Division, Library of Congress, Washington, D.C.
    William Jennings Bryan Papers

Southern Baptist Historical Library and Archives, Nashville, Tennessee
    Amzi Clarence Dixon Papers
    J. Frank Norris Papers

State Historical Society of Wisconsin, Madison, Wisconsin
    Bruce Barton Papers

Montgomery Library Archives, Westminster Theological Seminary, Philadelphia, Pennsylvania
   J. Gresham Machen Papers

Wheaton College Archives, Buswell Library, Wheaton College, Wheaton, Illinois
   Charles Blanchard Papers
   James Oliver Buswell Papers
   "Centennial Notebook"

Books, Essays, Theses, and Dissertations

Allen, Frederick Lewis. *Only Yesterday: An Informal History of the Nineteen-Twenties.* New York: Harper and Row, 1931.

Ammerman, Nancy T. "The Dynamics of Christian Fundamentalism: An Introduction." In *Accounting for Fundamentalisms: The Dynamic Character of Movements.* Vol. 4, *The Fundamentalism Project,* ed. Martin E. Marty and R. Scott Appleby. Chicago: Univ. of Chicago Press, 1994.

———. "North American Protestant Fundamentalism." In *Fundamentalisms Observed.* Vol. 1, *The Fundamentalism Project,* ed. Martin E. Marty and R. Scott Appleby. Chicago: Univ. of Chicago Press, 1991.

Barton, Bruce. *The Man Nobody Knows: A Discovery of the Real Jesus.* Indianapolis: Bobbs-Merrill, 1925.

Beale, David O. *In Pursuit of Purity: American Fundamentalism since 1850.* Greenville, S.C.: Unusual Publications, 1986.

Bendroth, Margaret Lamberts. *Fundamentalism and Gender, 1875 to the Present.* New Haven: Yale Univ. Press, 1993.

Blanchard, Charles A. *President Blanchard's Autobiography.* Boone, Iowa: Western Christian Alliance, 1915.

Blumhofer, Edith L. *Aimee Semple McPherson: Everybody's Sister.* Grand Rapids, Mich.: William B. Eerdmans, 1993.

Brereton, Virginia Lieson. *Training God's Army: The American Bible School, 1880–1940.* Bloomington: Indiana Univ. Press, 1990.

Buswell, J. Oliver, Jr. *The Lamb of God.* Vol. 4. Grand Rapids, Mich.: Zondervan, 1937.

Campbell, Colin. *The Romantic Ethic and the Spirit of Modern Consumerism.* New York: Basil Blackwell, 1987.

Carpenter, Joel A. *Revive Us Again: The Reawakening of American Fundamentalism.* New York: Oxford Univ. Press, 1997.

———. "Shelter in the Time of Storm: Fundamentalist Institutions and the Rise of Evangelical Protestantism, 1929–1942." *Church History* 49 (March 1980): 62–75.

Carter, Paul A. "The Fundamentalist Defense of the Faith." In *Change and Continuity in Twentieth-Century America: The 1920s,* ed. John Braeman, Robert H. Bremner, and David Brody. Columbus: Ohio State Univ. Press, 1968.

Carwardine, Richard. "'Antinomians' and 'Arminians': Methodists and the Market Revolution." In *The Market Revolution in America: Social, Political, and Religious Expressions, 1800–1880,* ed. Melvyn Stokes and Stephen Conway. Charlottesville: Univ. Press of Virginia, 1996.

Chernow, Ron. *Titan: The Life of John D. Rockefeller, Sr.* New York: Random House, 1998.

Clapp, Rodney. "Why the Devil Takes Visa." *Christianity Today* 40 (7 Oct. 1996): 19–33.

Coben, Stanley. *Rebellion against Victorianism: The Impetus for Cultural Change in 1920s America.* New York: Oxford Univ. Press, 1991.

Cochran, Thomas C. *Challenges to American Values: Society, Business, and Religion.* New York: Oxford Univ. Press, 1985.

Cox, Harvey. "The Warring Visions of the Religious Right." *Atlantic Monthly* 277 (Nov. 1995): 58–69.

Curtis, Susan. *A Consuming Faith: The Social Gospel and Modern American Culture.* Baltimore: Johns Hopkins Univ. Press, 1991.

Dalhouse, Mark Taylor. *An Island in the Lake of Fire: Bob Jones University, Fundamentalism, and the Separatist Movement.* Athens: Univ. of Georgia Press, 1996.

DeBerg, Betty A. *Ungodly Women: Gender and the First Wave of American Fundamentalism.* Minneapolis: Fortress Press, 1990.

Dixon, A. C. *Present Day Life and Religion: A Series of Sermons on Cardinal Doctrines and Popular Sins.* Chicago: Bible Institute Colportage Association, 1905.

Dorsett, Lyle W. *Billy Sunday and the Redemption of Urban America.* Grand Rapids, Mich.: William B. Eerdmans, 1991.

Dumenil, Lynn. *The Modern Temper: American Culture and Society in the 1920s.* New York: Hill and Wang, 1995.

Ershkowitz, Herbert. *John Wanamaker: Philadelphia Merchant.* Pennsylvania: Combined, 1999.

Eskridge, Larry. "Campus Life." In *Popular Religious Magazines of the United*

States, ed. P. Mark Fackler and Charles H. Lippy. Westport, Conn.: Greenwood Press, 1995.

Felski, Rita. *The Gender of Modernity.* Cambridge: Harvard Univ. Press, 1995.

Fox, Richard Wrightman, and T. J. Jackson Lears. Introduction. In *The Culture of Consumption: Critical Essays in American History, 1880–1980,* ed. Richard Wrightman Fox and T. J. Jackson Lears. New York: Pantheon Books, 1983.

Frank, Douglas. *Less than Conquerors: How Evangelicals Entered the Twentieth Century.* Grand Rapids, Mich.: William B. Eerdmans, 1986.

Furniss, Norman F. *The Fundamentalist Controversy, 1918–1931.* New Haven: Yale Univ. Press, 1954.

Gaebelein, Arno Clemens. *The Christ We Know: Meditations on the Person and Glory of Our Lord Jesus Christ.* New York: "Our Hope," 1927.

Gilbert, James. *Perfect Cities: Chicago's Utopias of 1893.* Chicago: Univ. of Chicago Press, 1991.

Goff, Philip. "'We Have Heard the Joyful Sound': Charles E. Fuller's Radio Broadcast and the Rise of Modern Evangelicalism." *Religion and American Culture* 9 (winter 1999): 67–95.

Gorman, Paul R. *Left Intellectuals and Popular Culture in Twentieth-Century America.* Chapel Hill: Univ. of North Carolina Press, 1996.

Graham, Billy. *Just As I Am: The Autobiography of Billy Graham.* San Francisco: Harper and Zondervan, 1997.

Gray, James M. *Great Epochs of Sacred History and the Shadows They Cast.* Chicago: Bible Institute Colportage Association, [1910].

———. *Prophecy and the Lord's Return: A Collection of Popular Articles and Addresses.* New York: Fleming H. Revell, 1917.

Green, Marty Nesselbush. "From Sainthood to Submission: Gender Images in Conservative Protestantism, 1900–1940." *Historian* 58 (spring 1996): 539–56.

Hamilton, Michael S. "The Fundamentalist Harvard: Wheaton College and the Continuing Vitality of American Evangelicalism, 1919–1965." Ph.D. diss., University of Notre Dame, 1994.

———. "Women, Public Ministry, and American Fundamentalism, 1920–1950." *Religion and American Culture* 3 (summer 1993): 171–96.

Hankins, Barry. *God's Rascal: J. Frank Norris and the Beginnings of Southern Fundamentalism.* Lexington: Univ. Press of Kentucky, 1996.

———. "Saving America: Fundamentalism and Politics in the Life of J. Frank Norris." Ph.D. diss., Kansas State University, 1990.

Hart, D. G. *Defending the Faith: J. Gresham Machen and the Crisis of Conservative Protestantism in Modern America*. Baltimore: Johns Hopkins Univ. Press, 1994.

Harvey, Paul. *Redeeming the South: Religious Cultures and Racial Identities among Southern Baptists, 1865–1925*. Chapel Hill: Univ. of North Carolina Press, 1997.

Haskell, Molly. "Movies and the Selling of Desire." In *Consuming Desires: Consumption, Culture, and the Pursuit of Happiness,* ed. Roger Rosenblatt. Washington, D.C.: Island Press, 1999.

Hassey, Janette. *No Time for Silence: Evangelical Women in Public Ministry around the Turn of the Century*. Grand Rapids, Mich.: Zondervan, 1986.

Hofstadter, Richard. *Anti-intellectualism in American Life*. New York: Alfred A. Knopf, 1963.

Horowitz, David A. "An Alliance of Convenience: Independent Exhibitors and Purity Crusaders Battle Hollywood, 1920–1940." *Historian* 59 (spring 1997): 553–72.

Hulse, Cy. "The Shaping of a Fundamentalist: A Case Study of Charles Blanchard." Master's thesis, Trinity Evangelical Divinity School, 1977.

Hunter, James Davison. *American Evangelicalism: Conservative Religion and the Quandary of Modernity*. New Brunswick, N.J.: Rutgers Univ. Press, 1983.

Iannaccone, Laurence R. "Heirs to the Protestant Ethic? The Economics of American Fundamentalists." In *Fundamentalisms and the State: Remaking Polities, Economies, and Militance*. Vol. 3 of *The Fundamentalism Project,* ed. Martin E. Marty and R. Scott Appleby. Chicago: Univ. of Chicago Press, 1993.

Ironside, H. A. *Miscellaneous Papers*. Vol. 2. New York: Loizeaux Brothers, 1945.

Jones, Bob [Jr.]. *Cornbread and Caviar: Reminiscences and Reflections*. Greenville, S.C.: Bob Jones University Press, 1985.

Jones, Bob [Sr.]. *Bob Jones' Revival Sermons*. Wheaton, Ill.: Sword of the Lord, 1948.

———. *Bob Jones' Sermons*. Montgomery, Ala.: State Press, 1908. Reprint, 1983.

———. *Comments on Here and Hereafter*. New York: Loizeaux Brothers, 1946.

———. *"My Friends."* Greenville, S.C.: Bob Jones Univ. Press, 1983.

———. *The Perils of America, or Where Are We Headed?* [Privately printed], 1934.

———. *Things I Have Learned: Chapel Talks at Bob Jones College.* [Privately printed], 1944.

———. *Two Sermons to Men: Sowing and Reaping, and You Can't Beat the Game.* Chicago: Glad Tidings, 1923.

———. *The Unbeatable Game: A Sermon to Men.* [Privately printed].

Kammen, Michael. *American Culture, American Tastes: Social Change and the 20th Century.* New York: Alfred A. Knopf, 1999.

Lambert, Frank. *"Pedlar in Divinity": George Whitefield and the Transatlantic Revivals, 1737–1770.* Princeton: Princeton Univ. Press, 1994.

Larson, Edward J. *Summer for the Gods: The Scopes Trial and America's Continuing Debate over Science and Religion.* New York: Basic Books, 1997.

Lears, T. J. Jackson. "From Salvation to Self Realization: Advertising and the Therapeutic Roots of the Consumer Culture, 1880–1930." In *The Culture of Consumption,* ed. Richard Wrightman Fox and T. J. Jackson Lears. New York: Pantheon Books, 1983.

———. *No Place of Grace: Antimodernism and the Transformation of American Culture, 1880–1920.* New York: Pantheon Books, 1981.

Longfield, Bradley J. *The Presbyterian Controversy: Fundamentalists, Modernists, and Moderates.* New York: Oxford Univ. Press, 1991.

Lundén, Rolf. *Business and Religion in the American 1920s.* New York: Greenwood Press, 1988.

MacLean, Nancy. *Behind the Mask of Chivalry: The Making of the Second Ku Klux Klan.* New York: Oxford Univ. Press, 1994.

Marsden, George M. "Evangelicals, History and Modernity." In *Evangelicalism and Modern America,* ed. George M. Marsden. Grand Rapids, Mich.: William B. Eerdmans, 1984.

———. *Fundamentalism and American Culture: The Shaping of Twentieth-Century Evangelicalism, 1870–1925.* New York: Oxford Univ. Press, 1980.

Marty, Martin E. "Equipoise." In *Consuming Desires,* ed. Roger Rosenblatt. Washington, D.C.: Island Press, 1999.

———. *The Irony of It All, 1893–1919.* Chicago: Univ. of Chicago Press, 1986.

———. *The Noise of Conflict, 1919–1941.* Chicago: Univ. of Chicago Press, 1991.

Marty, Martin E., and R. Scott Appleby, eds. *The Fundamentalism Project.* 5 vols. Chicago: Univ. of Chicago Press, 1991–95.

Massee, J. C. *Evangelistic Sermons.* New York: Fleming H. Revell, 1926.

———. *The Gospel in the Ten Commandments.* Butler, Ind.: Higley Press, [1922?].

———. *Rekindling the Pentecostal Fire.* 3d ed. Butler, Ind.: Higley Press, 1930.

———. *Sunday Night Talks.* Chicago: Bible Institute Colportage Association, 1926.

McDannell, Colleen. *Material Christianity: Religions and Popular Culture in America.* New Haven: Yale Univ. Press, 1995.

Miller, Robert Moats. *American Protestantism and Social Issues, 1919–1939.* Chapel Hill: Univ. of North Carolina Press, 1958.

———. *Harry Emerson Fosdick: Preacher, Pastor, Prophet.* New York: Oxford Univ. Press, 1985.

Moore, R. Laurence. *Selling God: American Religion in the Marketplace of Culture.* New York: Oxford Univ. Press, 1994.

Mouw, Richard J. *Consulting the Faithful: What Christian Intellectuals Can Learn from Popular Religion.* Grand Rapids, Mich.: William B. Eerdmans, 1994.

Niebuhr, H. Richard. *Christ and Culture.* New York: Harper and Brothers, 1951.

Noll, Mark A. *A History of Christianity in the United States and Canada.* Grand Rapids, Mich.: William B. Eerdmans, 1992.

Oberdeck, Kathryn J. *The Evangelist and the Impresario: Religion, Entertainment, and Cultural Politics in America, 1884–1914.* Baltimore: Johns Hopkins Univ. Press, 1999.

Ownby, Ted. *American Dreams in Mississippi: Consumers, Poverty and Culture, 1830–1998.* Chapel Hill: Univ. of North Carolina Press, 1999.

———. "Mass Culture, Upper-Class Culture, and the Decline of Church Discipline in the Evangelical South: The 1910 Case of the Godbold Mineral Well Hotel." *Religion and American Culture* 4 (winter 1994): 107–32.

———. *Subduing Satan: Religion, Recreation, and Manhood in the Rural South, 1865–1920.* Chapel Hill: Univ. of North Carolina Press, 1990.

Parrish, Michael E. *Anxious Decades: America in Prosperity and Depression, 1920–1941.* New York: W. W. Norton, 1992.

Pease, Otis. *The Responsibilities of American Advertising: Private Control and Public Influence, 1920–1940.* New Haven: Yale Univ. Press, 1958.

Perrett, Geoffrey. *America in the Twenties: A History.* New York: Simon and Schuster, 1982.

Quiggle, Gregg. "Moody Magazine." In *Popular Religious Magazines of the United States,* ed. P. Mark Fackler and Charles H. Lippy. Westport, Conn.: Greenwood Press, 1995.

Rausch, David A. *Arno C. Gaebelein, 1861–1945: Irenic Fundamentalist and Scholar.* New York: Edwin Mellen Press, 1983.

Reynolds, David S. *Walt Whitman's America: A Cultural Biography.* New York: Alfred A. Knopf, 1995.

Ribuffo, Leo P. *The Old Christian Right: The Protestant Far Right from the Great Depression to the Cold War.* Philadelphia: Temple Univ. Press, 1983.

Riley, William Bell. *The Crisis of the Church.* New York: Charles C. Cook, 1914.

———. *The Menace of Modernism.* New York: Christian Alliance, 1917.

———. *Messages for the Metropolis.* Chicago: Winona, 1906.

———. *Pastoral Problems.* New York: Fleming H. Revell, 1936.

———. *The Philosophies of Father Coughlin: Four Sermons.* Grand Rapids, Mich.: Zondervan, 1935.

———. *Problems of Youth.* Grand Rapids, Mich.: Zondervan, 1941.

———. *Revival Sermons: Essentials in Effective Evangelism.* New York: Fleming H. Revell, 1929.

———. *Wives of the Bible: A Cross-section of Femininity.* Grand Rapids, Mich.: Zondervan, 1938.

———. *Youth's Victory Lies This Way.* Grand Rapids, Mich.: Zondervan, 1936.

Romanowski, William D. *Pop Culture Wars: Religion and the Role of Entertainment in American Life.* Downers Grove, Ill.: InterVarsity Press, 1996.

Rosenblatt, Roger. Introduction. In *Consuming Desires: Consumption, Culture, and the Pursuit of Happiness,* ed. Roger Rosenblatt. Washington, D.C.: Island Press, 1999.

Russell, C. Allyn. *Voices of American Fundamentalism.* Philadelphia: Westminster Press, 1976.

Sandeen, Ernest R. *The Roots of Fundamentalism: British and American Millenarianism, 1800–1930.* Chicago: Univ. of Chicago Press, 1970.

Schmidt, Leigh Eric. *Consumer Rites: The Buying and Selling of American Holidays.* Princeton: Princeton Univ. Press, 1995.

Schor, Juliet. "What's Wrong with Consumer Society." In *Consuming Desires: Consumption, Culture, and the Pursuit of Happiness,* ed. Roger Rosenblatt. Washington, D.C.: Island Press, 1999.

Shuler, R. P. *Bob Shuler Met These on the Trail.* Wheaton, Ill.: Sword of the Lord, 1955.

———. *What New Doctrine Is This?* New York: Abingdon-Cokesbury Press, 1946.

Sidwell, Mark Edward. "The History of the Winona Lake Bible Conference." Ph.D. diss., Bob Jones University, 1988.

Smith, Gary Scott. *The Seeds of Secularization: Calvinism, Culture, and Plural-*

ism in America, 1870–1915. Grand Rapids, Mich.: Christian Univ. Press, 1985.

Still, Mark Sumner. "'Fighting Bob' Shuler: Fundamentalist and Reformer." Ph.D. diss., Claremont Graduate School, 1988.

Stout, Harry S. *The Divine Dramatist: George Whitefield and the Rise of Modern Evangelicalism.* Grand Rapids, Mich.: William B. Eerdmans, 1991.

Straton, John Roach. *Fighting the Devil in Modern Babylon.* Boston: Stratford, 1929.

———. *The Gardens of Life: Messages of Cheer and Comfort.* New York: George H. Doran, 1921.

———. *The Menace of Immorality in Church and State: Messages of Wrath and Judgment.* New York: George H. Doran, 1920.

Susman, Warren I. *Culture As History: The Transformation of American Society in the Twentieth Century.* New York: Pantheon Books, 1984.

Tindall, George Brown, with David E. Shi. *America: A Narrative History.* Vol. 2, 3d ed. New York: W. W. Norton, 1992.

Torrey, R. A. *The God of the Bible.* New York: George H. Doran, 1923.

———. *The Gospel for Today: New Evangelistic Sermons for a New Day.* New York: Fleming H. Revell, 1922.

Trollinger, William Vance, Jr. *God's Empire: William Bell Riley and Midwestern Fundamentalism.* Madison: Univ. of Wisconsin Press, 1990.

Trumbull, Charles G. *Prophecy's Light on Today.* New York: Fleming H. Revell, 1937.

———. *Victory in Christ.* Ft. Washington, Pa.: Christian Literature Crusade, 1959.

Turner, Daniel Lynn. "Fundamentalism, the Arts, and Personal Refinement: A Study of the Ideals of Bob Jones, Sr. and Bob Jones, Jr." Ed.D. diss., University of Illinois at Urbana-Champaign, 1988.

Wagner, Ann. *Adversaries of Dance: From Puritans to the Present.* Urbana: Univ. of Illinois Press, 1997.

Watt, David Harrington. *A Transforming Faith: Explorations of Twentieth-Century American Evangelicalism.* New Brunswick, N.J.: Rutgers Univ. Press, 1991.

Wauzzinski, Robert A. *Between God and Gold: Protestant Evangelicalism and the Industrial Revolution, 1820–1914.* Rutherford, N.J.: Fairleigh Dickinson Univ. Press, 1993.

Wenger, Robert E. "Social Thought in American Fundamentalism, 1918–1933." Ph.D. diss., University of Nebraska, 1973.

Wosh, Peter J. *Spreading the Word: The Bible Business in Nineteenth-Century America*. Ithaca: Cornell Univ. Press, 1994.

Wuthnow, Robert. *God and Mammon in America*. New York: Free Press, 1994.

———. *The Struggle for America's Soul: Evangelicals, Liberals, and Secularism*. Grand Rapids, Mich.: William B. Eerdmans, 1989.

Index